Thursday's Bird

Thursday's Bird

Hunting Wild Pheasants in a Vanishing Upland

by
Joel Spring

SAFARI PRESS INC.

Spring, Joel.

First edition

Safari Press Inc.

2003, Long Beach, California

ISBN 1-57157-259-7

Library of Congress Catalog Card Number: 2002105000

10 9 8 7 6 5 4 3 2 1

Readers wishing to receive the Safari Press catalog, featuring many fine books on big-game hunting, wingshooting, and sporting firearms, should write to Safari Press Inc., P.O. Box 3095, Long Beach, CA 90803, USA. Tel: (714) 894-9080 or visit our Web site at www.safaripress.com.

This book is fondly dedicated to anyone—four-legged or two—who has ever spent the day chasing wild birds with me. There may have been more days without birds than with, but I wouldn't change the memories we've made for anything.

TABLE OF CONTENTS

INTRODUCTION

I've heard of areas where you can go to shoot pheasants, lots of them, and they aren't all that hard to find. These stories, secondhand accounts for the most part, tell of counties and even states so full of birds that you can see hundreds in a day, even over an average bird dog. I find the tales hardly believable, but if these places do exist, they are far from here in Niagara County, New York. Some old-timers have told me the birdhunting around here used to be like that. I don't find that as hard to believe since, more often than not, my timing is terrible. I always arrive an hour after the free stuff has been given away, a day after the steelhead run has petered out, a week after the whitetail rut has peaked and all the deer have since gone into hiding; I show up on the stormy day after the month-long run of good weather—and so on, to a depressing degree. Even when it came to the year of my birth, as it related to the rise and fall of the western New York pheasant population, my timing was as bad as ever. That is to say, simply *terrible*.

I began hunting pheasants in the early 1990s, roughly fifteen years after the bulk of the wild ringnecks disappeared. When I finally got around to setting foot in the fields behind my first bird dog at age twenty-seven, most of the diehard pheasant hunters around here had given up altogether.

It was OK for a while, at least for the first couple of years. I still found pockets of wild birds through hard work, and occasionally my dogs and I even killed a limit of wild roosters. I was happy, for a while. Then the old-timers began talking. They'd see me out beating the brush with my dogs, Maggie and Ted, and they would stop in wonder.

"What the hell are you after, boy? Pheasants? No kidding? You should have been here twenty years ago."

As a matter of course, they'd proceed to tell me about going afield and shooting a limit of pheasants without a dog—of waiting by the roosting trees at dusk and selecting only the biggest cockbirds to shoot as dozens of birds winged their way past them toward the evening security provided by the thickets. Compared with my ground-covering days driven by hopes of flushing three or four birds, those old days must have been superb— or so they said. The simple truth is that I'd missed them by a mile—or a couple of decades anyway.

I could have hunted back then, mind you, since I was old enough in the late 1970s and early '80s. But my family did not hunt, and it wasn't until I met my future wife that I first picked up a shotgun and headed afield. Characteristically, my timing was way off. By the time I first followed in the wake of my eager bird dogs, Niagara County's pheasants had been corralled into a few small areas where the housing developments had not yet sprawled. Such places still exist, but we are losing them by the day. By the *hour*, it seems lately.

In addition to the development, farmers today practice "ditch-to-ditch" planting, eradicating most of the thick hedgerows that used to crisscross the countryside and are so necessary to support a healthy pheasant population in such heavily farmed land. Where there aren't new houses, there is corn, with scarcely a hedgerow in sight.

The birds I find now live in creek bottoms, where modern technology has not yet learned to plant a cornstalk. They live in the occasional forsaken farmstead, but most of those old plots have grown up so much now that the fields have reverted to woods. These are fine places for deer and rabbits and woodcock. And woodcock are fun, but they ain't pheasants.

The ringnecks we do find in the magical handful of locations I guard with great secrecy are wild and raucous and smart. (If asked ten years ago if a bird could really be "smart," I would have laughed you off the back porch, but now I know differently.) As a result, Maggie and Ted have become a proficient hunting team, having learned the hard way how to ferret out these wily, wild birds with a level of precision that I've seen in few other hunting dogs. Of course, they're *my* dogs, so my opinion might be just a tad skewed, but I can vouch for them. I have seen Maggie catch a wild rooster on the ground; I've seen Ted pin one against an old stone fence and not release it to flush until I was positioned to shoot. I have not seen many other dogs do these things. Those smart birds have made my dogs smart. Maggie and Ted work hard for me, so I treat them well by breaking the rules and letting them flush and retrieve rabbits and squirrels and crows and pigeons, to make up for the lack of pheasants. I let them hunt almost anything that is legal, just to keep their skills sharp. I know people will disagree with letting dogs "run fur," but Mag and Ted don't seem to mind.

So why, if these pheasants are so hard to come by and even harder to kill when we *do* finally come by them, do I deliberately take the last weeks in October and the first weeks in November year after year, expending precious vacation time and yet knowing I will end each week frustrated and tired without any guarantee of a single bird making its way to my freezer?

Why do I look forward to it for months, envisioning and obsessing, hoping and believing that this year will be better than the last, even when I know it probably will be worse?

If you have ever seen and heard the flush of a wild ringneck, you know why. If you've ever seen an exhausted dog drop a giant rooster at your feet, you'll understand. If you have been there and seen those things, there is probably no question in your mind.

In this book, I'm hoping to show you—and maybe explain to myself—what this madness is all about. Especially those of you who live in places like my bailiwick, where the city is edging out the country but a few of us still pull on brush pants and old coats and head afield each year with a pocket full of shells and a heart full of hope.

If by some chance you live in one of those enchanted places where huge flocks of pheasants block out the sun and fall easily to the gun, you are welcome to come along, too, but please keep your laughter down so the rest of us can enjoy ourselves.

Chapter One

Preparations

Lawns and Leaves

My lawn mower wasn't meant to go ninety miles an hour—a fact probably stated somewhere in the owner's manual (along with other nonsense about regularly changing the oil, undoubtedly) if I'd ever bothered to read it. But here's the thing—I just hate mowing. I merely *dislike* it in June, July, and August, when grass-growing season is at its peak. But when September and October roll around, any shred of patience I might have harbored for lawn care in the warmer months is long gone. Fall is for birdhunting and thinking about birdhunting, not for mowing the grass. So, to minimize this nuisance in the autumn months, I mow fast—really fast. I have never actually *rolled* the lawn mower *per se*, but I have strained the machine to the outer limits of its poorly engineered tolerances. Although, considering that the machine has held together for almost three years now—a record for lawn mowers under my watch—I suppose I shouldn't call it poorly engineered, but it's still a lawn mower, and how much good can you say about one?

Most of the limbs on the countless trees in my yard have been trimmed up to a sufficient height so I can race under them comfortably without banging my head. (This is done each spring by walking around the yard with my handsaw and looking for the low-hanging branches—it's easy to spot the ones in need of trimming by the large bloodstains on them.) This allows me to make good time in my mowing.

Thoughts about bird season made it maddening to be sitting astride the cursed machine instead of out scouting for woodcock only a few scant weeks before the season was to begin. I don't get as worked up about woodcock as I do about ringnecks, but they are at least something to wrap my mind around and supply a handy excuse to get the dogs back out working again. Even after the small-game season opens, my mind is not on squirrels or rabbits or, least of all, the mowing.

All I can think about are wild birds.

There is a lot to be said for being rich. I mean, I wouldn't personally *know,* but it must be nice. A life of leisure is often wasted on the wrong people, I think. I regularly have fantasies about hiring a lawn-care company to come in and do my yard work; I picture myself strolling across the lawn in my brush pants and hunting coat, dogs heeling obediently at my side (OK, so they never really do *that,* but this is a fantasy, after all), and waving casually to the yard men bustling about, trimming my bushes, cutting my grass, and, in the fall, raking my leaves. . . .

And don't even get me *started* about the leaves!

Why God decided to make leaves fall in the middle of . . . well . . . *fall,* I just cannot fathom. And the leaf fall is always deceptive. Sure, they turn yellow and red and brown, and a handful of them drift down from the treetops during the early parts of October. But during woodcock season, they mostly just *hang* up there. Then a strange thing happens, right about the third week in October when pheasant season opens: They stop falling. Honest. I've seen it. They just suspend in the treetops. Each year at that time I look up at them and think, *Good, this year they're just going to stay up there.* I go on about my business (which during the last half of October consists solely of sleeping, drinking coffee, and hunting pheasants) and try to ignore the leaves, as if thinking about them too much might just *cause* them to fall. Trudging in from the field at sunset each night, I eye the clumps of leaves high in the cottonwood trees surrounding my house, turning the spotlight on to inspect them, and note approvingly how few have dropped in the past day; then I go to bed. This process is repeated throughout the first week or so of pheasant season.

Then it happens.

One morning after a bit of windy overnight rain, usually sometime around Halloween, my kids and the dogs step off the back porch and disappear into a sea of leaves that is shoulder-high to a tall man. I rescue the children and pets by cutting a swath to them with the leaf blower, and bird season is suddenly put on hold. Once I'm certain the children are safe again, I bitterly set about clearing up the leaves.

So this past year, cruising around the yard on my smoking, clacking (oil, *schmoil*) lawnmower, I wasn't happy to be mowing, but at the same time the growth rate of my grass seemed finally to be slowing down. Maybe this year, it really wouldn't need mowing in October. *It's already the end of September*, I thought to myself—*maybe this is it!* Content in my own grand denial, I eyed the profusion of cottonwood leaves overhead. This time, they really did look like they were attached pretty well. Maybe, just maybe, they would stay up there, at least through bird season.

Hey, a guy can dream.

Eighty-two Acres

I thought crying in front of a perfect stranger probably would not be appropriate. He was nice enough, and I suppose it wasn't his fault. But then again, it *was.* . . .

I knew trouble was brewing last year, and when the "For Sale" signs went up on the property, a terrible feeling of dread assailed me. To the farmer selling it ("*Eighty-Two Acres—For Sale!*"), I'm sure it meant only some badly needed cash. The place had been untended for years, and in the farmer's mind may have been wasted land. Maybe it was beyond the old guy's means to clear the brush and the old vineyard posts and laboriously till it into something agriculturally useful. Each year, when I asked him if I might run the dogs for pheasants there, he always gave me a shrug as if he had forgotten about the place until I brought it to his attention.

As useless as it was to him, I don't think he ever imagined what delight the place brought to me. If the farmer *had* ever sunk a moment's thought into the times over the past six years when he spotted me running insanely around his property yelling and whistling for my dogs, flushing the occasional bird after hours of tramping in circles, then often missing it, he might have felt bad for me. Possibly he considered that selling off my pheasant-hunting grounds would have been doing me a favor: "*Maybe he'll find something more useful to do with his life than chasing those half-breed dogs all over Creation.*"

Maybe not.

Before I hunted the land, I was no stranger to it. Living in a duplex across the road for a time, I used to venture into the fields to escape the close confines of our small apartment. The old vineyards revealed many things on my walks. There were woodcock and pheasants, ducks in the two small irrigation ponds, turkeys, and deer. A shed pair of six-point antlers I found within sight of my bathroom window still hangs from a peg in my den. The rutted, neglected land was home to nearly every kind of game. At a time when the wild ringneck population had dropped precipitously, I regularly found pheasant nests on the high ground between the vineyard rows. Before I had dogs of my own, we used to hunt there over John's Labrador, Mike. Following the keen nose of the aging dog, we shot rabbits and pheasants, shot at zigzagging woodcock, and even took a couple mallards off the smaller of the two ponds one crisp autumn morning. Old Mike took his last pheasant on those eighty-two acres. (*For Sale!*)

Long after Mike was gone, Ted and Maggie learned their hunting craft on other pieces of land. The old vineyard hadn't seen my boot prints in a year or two when I finally returned one miserable rainy day. It seemed fitting when Ted flushed and retrieved his first rooster there.

Dogs and men move on, but I guess it is difficult to comprehend that something as seemingly permanent as a piece of land can move on, too. In those last years the pheasant hunting remained spectacular, rewarding us with big birds. At a time when my frustrated hunting acquaintances were swearing there wasn't a wild bird left in the county, this oasis consistently shared its wealth with us. We were taking birds in other places, top-secret caches of wild birds I am not at liberty to divulge, but this place (*For Sale—82 Acres*) became the crown jewel of our ringneck hunts.

I passed that damned sign driving to work each day for weeks, then months—as if I'd needed a reminder of the potential peril. For two years I watched the red-white-and-blue "For Sale" sign fade and rust. When grass sprouted up and finally towered over it, the realtor's telephone number seemed as forgotten as the land. My apprehension over losing my hunting grounds faded with the patriotic paint on the sign. But one steamy morning last August, I nearly wrecked my truck. One bright red word across the faded old sign made my heart sink.

"Sold!"

"Oh, no."

Rooster pheasant emerging from hedgerow.

OK, I rationalized, *so some developer has picked up the land. He'll make a grand plan to put a dozen or so houses on it. It will take years. With any luck it will fail miserably, like the rest of the small-time developments around here. I'll still be hunting this land ten years from now. No problem.*

My rationale seemed correct, and it helped me sleep at night. But a month later, again on my way to work, I was again blown out of the water. The little ramshackle house standing on a forgotten knoll at the south edge of the property was showing signs of life. It was hard for me to believe that the building—really nothing more than a shack—was worth saving. If my developer theory was right, they would bulldoze the place to make room for more lucrative housing. But on this still-warm morning, just into the first throes of the September goose season, what I saw amazed me.

Siding.

Boxes and boxes of vinyl siding laid out all around the house gave me an inkling of the bright blue shell that the shack was about to become. *Cancel that theory,* I thought. *A private homeowner has bought the whole shebang. OK,* I expertly rationalized once again, *I have a lot better chance of getting permission to hunt the property from a private homeowner than from some snooty big-city developer. Yes, someone who could appreciate this piece of property enough to buy it certainly could understand another person wanting to hunt here. I mean, eighty acres is plenty of land. Heck, they might even welcome a friendly face wandering around to keep an eye on the place.*

Not wanting to bother the new homeowner in the midst of his renovation, I continued watching the place. A week before pheasant season, the house was a hub

7

of activity. In the overgrown driveway, an electrical contractor's van sat with its doors flung wide like the flapping wings of a bird. On the roof, two men worked laying out tarpaper. Pallets of shingles sat around the house, waiting.

Standing back, not looking busy like the rest of them but surveying the home like a king might observe the stone blocks being placed around his new castle, was a young guy. His doughy face revealed nothing of his personality. His dress, jeans and a T-shirt much like my own, told me little about his politics or his views on hunting, two items that don't necessarily rely on one another. Pulling my own truck in the driveway to join the parade of home-improvement vehicles, I tried to judge the man, but it was useless. As I stepped out of the truck, he was suddenly right there, extending his hand and introducing himself.

Good, I thought. *Very good.*

His preemptive handshake was indicative of his personality, and I couldn't help liking the guy. It should not be rare that you run into nice folks out in the country, or anywhere else for that matter, but it seems increasingly the case that nobody wants anything to do with you if they haven't known you for ten years. This man was just a plain-old nice guy. Before he even knew why I was there, he offered me a drink, walked me around the house, and generally told me his life story. I complimented him on the purchase of the property and on the home improvements—I complimented everything I could possibly think of before popping the question.

"You know, I've hunted pheasants here for several years, and was wondering if I might get your permission to hunt here this year."

He looked off to the side, almost ashamed and visibly pained. My heart sank.

"Well . . . ." The words came hard to him. I could already see that no matter how well we hit it off, I wasn't going to shoot any birds here ever again. Never.

Damn.

"See, a friend of mine asked me if he could hunt here last week, and my wife went ballistic and said there will be *no* hunting on this property." Holding both hands out, he said, "I don't mind, personally, but I have to keep the peace, you know?"

"Sure, sure. I know." A stake through my heart would have been less painful. My distress must have been obvious—I don't know how it would not be.

"Sorry, man. I really am."

"No, that's all right. We have plenty of places to hunt."

Just one less now.

"If it makes you feel any better, there aren't hardly any pheasants out there anyway. Me and Sparky," he said, gesturing to the misshapen mutt suspiciously eyeing the siding crew, "walked the whole property twice now, and we only saw one bird. You're not missing out on much."

Now he was bearing down and really twisting that stake. *Hardly any pheasants?* I thought about getting my cell phone and putting 911 on speed-dial. My heart was fluttering in an unhealthy manner. *He's sitting on the single best pheasant acreage in the whole county and there are hardly any pheasants? Oh, you fool!*

"I see," I said, not seeing at all.

"Anyway, we're going to dig out the center of the property and put a thirty-acre pond in."

Enough! Stop!

"Oh, that'll be nice," I said.

Once back in my truck after handshakes and gentlemanly good-byes, I smacked the dashboard of my old truck, hard enough to change the radio station and make the dash lights flutter.

Lost another one.

Too Hot

It was too hot for this, too hot for *anything.* I hate when it happens like this. Autumn was rolling nicely along, the days ticking down toward pheasant season, the temperature dropping a few degrees every day and a few more degrees every night. Then it happened.

It got hot.

Tired of just sitting around and *thinking* about hunting, I took Maggie and Ted to one of our prime spots for wild pheasants. I waited for the kids to get on the bus, waving to them as they roared off in the big yellow tub, before letting the dogs out and beckoning them to the truck. I wasn't dressed in my hunting clothes, and they both eyed me suspiciously as they hopped into the truck—suspicious, I imagine, of a surprise trip to the vet. Once we neared the pheasant field, though, in the rearview I watched them pacing back and forth, whining and nipping playfully at each other. In the way of all the hunting dogs I have ever known, they knew where they were going and precisely what they were going to do—even if Master didn't have a gun or his hunting clothes but merely a camera.

Bursting from the back of the truck, the dogs were in the waist-high grass before I had my film loaded, and were fifty yards ahead of me before I even set foot into the cover. I let them go. After a few minutes of deranged ripping around the field, they settled into a pace, Ted quartering fifteen yards in front of me with Maggie running an opposite crossing pattern thirty yards out. Tugging at the camera strap around my neck, I longed for my shotgun.

Not even the heat could take away the anticipation.

Without the benefit of the first hard frost, the grass rose thick and tall, and when Maggie swung back close to check on me, she sported a cloak of briars and burrs. It would take hours to comb her out. She didn't seem to mind, though, bouncing through the fields with unbridled glee.

A hundred yards in, Ted flushed a rabbit across my feet and briefly chased it before realizing I wasn't going to shoot it. It was too hot, though, and he didn't pursue it with any dedication. I could have brought the shotgun—rabbits were legal now—but the 80-degree day just did not put me in the mood. Besides, rabbits are usually little more than a V-shaped wake in the grass at this time of the year. Of course, this one would have been a cinch.

Focusing my attention, and my camera, on Ted, whose tongue drooped to the ground as if it had been disconnected at the base, I failed to notice Maggie—or, more accurately, the *lack* of Maggie. After snapping a quick picture of the at-once goofy and regal Ted, I heard her snorting upfield from me. Standing on my tiptoes atop one of the overgrown ruts from the field's long-gone days as farmland, I finally spotted her, a brown-and-white blur racing dead away from me with her nose to the ground. Ted, whose ears are far better than mine, heard her trademark snorting and rushed after her. Certain of her ability to ferret out fresh scent, he didn't even bother to stop and check it for himself. Just as Ted caught up with Maggie—with me still forty yards behind and hurrying as fast as I could through the long grass—a rooster flushed wild a good fifty yards ahead of the dogs. I raised the camera and fumbled with the zoom lens, managing to get two photos before the bird disappeared into an adjacent cornfield. Maggie, who would normally have raced after the bird—a trait I've never been able to break her of but know I should—flopped to the ground, overheated but smiling. Ted lay down next to her.

"You've got to flush them a little closer than that, Mag. I couldn't have shot that one."

She looked at me, cocking her head slightly before dismissing my commentary and rising to her feet. Just like that, she went back at it. I love Maggie. Ted followed on my heels for a few moments, catching his breath before deciding Maggie must be having all the fun and charging after her.

We walked the length of the big field and flushed another rabbit—or at least that's what I assumed it was from the halfhearted chase the dogs gave. Turning back toward the road, I smiled, pleased to have seen one bird but lamenting that it was smart enough to escape unharmed. Like the vast majority of the wild birds we'd taken there, it would not have been an easy one. Had it been hunting season, we might have chased it into the cornfield and flushed it two or three more times before it finally came up close enough for a shot. There is just nothing easy about wild ringnecks. They are hard to find and even harder to kill.

That's OK, though, because that is why we like them.

Halfway back to the truck, Ted made a hard right turn into a dogwood hedgerow, a thick maroon border separating the field from an adjacent bean field. A moment later, with Maggie now lagging by my side, a huge cockbird rose squawking and cackling as it beat its wings trying to escape the hedgerow and Ted's jaws. In its desperate ascent, the rooster failed to recognize the danger only five yards away. For a frozen moment as it gained height, the bird's feathers stood out in the polarized light of morning. Tail feathers drooped as wings beat upward. Its eye reflected the day's new sun. I could have reached out and touched it.

I ducked as it flew right over me.

Maggie made a short dash across the field but seemed to know that if I was not going to shoot, it wasn't worth the effort of another sweltering cross-country run. The bird soared across the long grass and settled into the corn, in precisely the same spot the other rooster had. In this veritable sea of stalks, it seemed noteworthy that both birds selected the same area in which to land. I suspected that a ditch or an open patch in the corn drew them there and triangulated the place in my mind.

I would be coming back to that spot very soon— *with* a shotgun.

The dogs took the lead, ranging perhaps a little too far out, but I didn't blame them. The field crackled dry and hot under their feet, and the dogs knew a cooler full of ice water awaited them at the tailgate of the truck. I let them go and turned once more to look at the place where the birds had landed, trying to burn the exact location into my mind.

Suddenly remembering my camera, I realized I had just missed one hell of a photo: a ringneck in prime morning light, the red of the dogwoods, the gold of the fields. It was not the first time I'd blown a great shot, and it certainly wouldn't be the last. Besides, after that encounter my mind busied itself considering things other than photography—namely, two large rooster pheasants. Smiling with the devious satisfaction of a sniper who has walked for weeks through miles of hostile territory and finally sighted his target, I hiked slowly back to the truck, soaked in sweat but savoring the day.

Driving home with the fresh memory of the two birds, I played back the morning's scenes in my mind, especially the second flush. He would have been an easy shot, a rare occurrence in our pursuit of wild pheasants, and one of those instances where the bird came up so close I would've had to let him get out a few more yards before shooting. *Chalk one up for Ted.*

I envisioned the way Ted trotted along the hedgerow, tired from the heat and probably eager just to get back to the truck. But when he hit that pheasant scent, it was as if he had smacked into a brick wall. Perhaps that's not the best way to describe it. Maybe I should just borrow a phrase from a friend and call it Lab Radar. It fits. While Maggie tends to course quickly back and forth sniffing for ground scent, Ted trots along at his own slow pace, at times exasperating me with his carefree appearance. Unlike Maggie, who busts brush and covers more ground than Ted and I combined, he will often stay in a straight line in front of us, especially if we are quartering into the wind, and let the breeze do the job for him. His big, blocky head swings slowly back and forth, and his nose is working, but he is the picture of relaxation. The first few times we took him afield, I stayed after him, directing him into the brush with a harsh word and a pointed finger, expecting him to act like Maggie. But after his first few pheasant flushes I realized that, like Maggie, he was *always* working. The Lab Radar is always up and receiving.

Once, after a grueling hunt in Genesee County, Ted seemed overheated and was not acting normally. I had seen a friend's Lab collapse from the heat in that same spot—the sawgrass and multiflora rose were extraordinarily thick there—and I decided to call off hunting and get Ted down to the creek for a drink and a swim to cool off. I was worried about him. The day

Author and Ted with cornfield rooster.

had climbed from a comfortable 55 degrees to a nearly unbearable 80 degrees in a few hours, and even though he flushed a pair of pheasants to the guns, Ted just wasn't himself. As we walked down the trail toward the creek, his tongue dragged the ground, and he moved with a slow, swerving gait, like an old pickup truck with a bad steering column. As we neared the creek, about where I expected him to break and run for the relief of the cold water, Ted stopped dead in the trail and stared hard at the brush to his left. A thin screen of thorny multiflora rose bordered an old stone fence. My two hunting companions flanked Ted and me and looked to see what he had smelled. There wasn't much cover, and a bird would have been obvious. It was probably either a woodcock or a cottontail, something with good camouflage and the willingness to sit tight, we decided. With his nose in the air and sniffing madly, tuning in that Lab Radar, Ted examined the situation closely. Just as I debated ordering him into the prickly brush, he went on his own. But instead of working along the stone fence, in a single bound he jumped over it, surprising the hell out of the pheasant huddled against the other side. The bird came up so fast and so hard that it took a moment for two of us to get our guns up. We didn't blame Ted when he ran past the dead bird instead of retrieving it and flung himself into the cool water of the creek.

Lab Radar is also what makes Ted such an effective woodcock killer. While Maggie busts brush at heart-stopping speed and puts up pheasants more regularly than Ted, there is seldom even scant warning that a timberdoodle is about to flush. Ted stays close to the hunters and, if Maggie hasn't already put up the birds ahead of us, will often flush woodcock within easy shooting range . . . not that any woodcock shooting is easy. Ted's head swings slowly back and forth, and once the radar picks up a bird, he will lock up for a split second in a half-baked point before lowering his broad head and charging into the cover like a bulldozer. In that split second it is wise to have your thumb on the safety and your eyes and ears on full alert because something is going to flush.

When Ted gets excited, you know something is about to happen, because the game he picks up on his radar screen is usually quite close. Maggie, on the other hand, is the ground-scenter. She simply makes things happen. I have seen her unravel scent trails for a hundred yards, huffing and snorting and, most importantly, *thinking.* Many times she has been working a line of hot pheasant scent, only to give it up and dash directly into a patch of cover where the bird was likely headed. She has a knack for outthinking wild rooster pheasants. It is a wonderful trait in a bird dog, because those birds want to stay running on the ground. They want a foot chase, and if you don't cut them off, eventually you'll probably either get a wild flush or run yourself and your dogs into exhaustion.

That's what the birds hope for, I'm sure.

While Ted has his radar, Maggie has her own high-tech equipment in the form of a refined scent-imaging system. That's how I think of it anyway. It's amazing to watch her hit a fresh scent: At first she works it back and forth, to see which direction it's heading—that she can figure it out alone amazes me—and then she begins the pursuit. If the trail is several hours old, she will still work it, but leisurely, opting for a fresher trail if we should come across one. But when she is on hot scent, watch out. I have several ruined boots and pairs of brush pants that attest to chasing after Maggie when she's birdy. Even after a long, hot, grueling, all-day hunt, she has a hidden reserve of adrenaline that she taps into when a bird is nearby. She seems to understand the necessity of getting on the bird and flushing it fast before it has a chance to run. When she really gets going, she begins a harsh huffing and snorting that you can hear from a hundred yards away. The noise is often helpful in locating her because she usually stops listening to me at those times. She becomes so engrossed in the scent and the proximity of the bird that she ignores calls and hand signals. This is usually fine, and I am pleased she is so dedicated to her task, but there are times when things get frustrating for the slower, two-legged hunters in Maggie's company. Several times she has crossed a barrier like a deep creek or an all-but-impenetrable hedgerow and continued chasing the bird long after we mere humans were eating her dust. I attribute it to her lack of good training, but I still admire her tenacity. Nine times out of ten she will flush the bird, just not always within gun range. I can't tell you the times she's looked back at me after one of those wild flushes as if to say, *"Why didn't you shoot?. . . Oh, you're way back there!"* It's frustrating, but it's the same killer instinct that has put many birds in my freezer over the last seven years.

In a place where I am apt to run into other hunters or the cover is too thick to keep track of two dogs, I enjoy hunting just one of my pair, but they truly excel as a team. They have evolved a dynamic partnership over the past few years. Ted works close as always, checking the wind, while Maggie quarters restlessly, scanning the ground for scent. Ted has learned that when Maggie begins her sniffing and snorting routine, it's time to run over and see what she is after. Maggie has learned to read Ted's body language as well. She knows that when he stops looking goofy and starts looking serious, it's time to check him out. Often the dogs will try to outthink each other. If we are working into the wind and Ted picks up scent, Maggie will race ahead of him twenty or thirty yards. This has resulted in many birds getting cut off between them and forced into the air for a shot. I have no doubt that by working as a team they have saved us some long down-field runs after wild pheasants.

After the shot, the retrieve used to be something of a competition, each dog trying to beat the other to the downed bird. But after several all-out brawls over a dead bird, Ted will usually leave the bird to Maggie in the interest of family peace, unless it happens to fall right at his feet. Yes, I have an eighty-five-pound retriever that surrenders the bird cleanup duty to a forty-pound springer. Ted is a fine retriever when he is hunting alone with me, but when Maggie is along, he barely tries anymore, not wishing to spark her Tasmanian Devil-like temper. I don't blame him.

In the bed of the truck, both dogs panted hard but were finally relaxed, curled up on the old blanket. Ted's head rested across Maggie's back, his favorite pillow. All in all, not a bad team. I couldn't wait to see them in real action again.

Threshold

I wasn't sure I could really see my breath, but I thought I could. I wanted to, anyway. Fall had been a long time coming, and now I stood on its threshold, trying to make it come even faster, fearless of the long winter that would follow close behind and fully focused on the joy of the coming weeks.

I'd brought the .22 rifle almost as an afterthought. A squirrel had not crossed my path since early on when an almost comically fat one ran frantically out ahead of me on the logging road, zigzagging from the imagined danger of my slow-moving, old ATV. The puttering old Honda always seems an affront to the peaceful woods, but this place was far from home, and I had only an hour before dark. The machine was quiet enough, but I was glad to be off it and moving in the footsteps of wild things instead of in tire tracks.

I had spent the past forty minutes carefully skirting the area I would be bowhunting for deer in a few short weeks. I was anxious to scout the area but had no desire to spook the deer around my newly constructed tree stand. As it often does, however, my curiosity got the better of me, and I found my worn hunting boots pointed in the direction of the tree stand. Without a squirrel to distract me, I tried to keep my footfalls quiet in the crisp carpet of last year's fallen leaves. When I found myself hurrying, I slowed down and simply listened, a luxury the frantic events of the past week hadn't allowed me. In fact, I could not remember the last time I'd just sat and listened. My best guess would be last fall, and that was a shame.

Finding a large log, still several hundred yards from my stand, I lowered myself and sat against it, trying to ignore the mossy dampness leaching through my shirt and into my lower back. To my right I sensed blurred movement in the dimming light—a gray squirrel running with a hickory nut in his mouth. Racing up a sapling twenty yards from me, he turned and hung from his hind legs, intent on devouring the nut, carefully held like a miniature basketball between his front paws. Seeing a flash off my gun barrel as I moved to put him in my sights, he raced up the tree, flinging himself through the adjoining treetops with abandon. My last glimpse showed him forty feet above the forest floor, the large hickory nut tucked firmly back in his jaws. Then he melted into the darkening green canopy. The whole encounter lasted no more than a minute, but the light had dimmed perceptibly in that short time.

Like autumn, nightfall comes on fast once its mind is made up.

It was still a good walk to the tree stand, but I had no desire to reach it in the dark when I would most likely encounter the neighborhood deer, including one spectacular eight-point buck that had been feeding around the base of the tree where my stand resides. I sated my curiosity a bit by walking as far as the nearby deer runway leading down to my stand. The deer sign was thick and fresh in the black mud of a low spot in the trail.

Smiling to myself, I headed back out of the woods, shortcutting in hopes of making it back to the Honda by dark. No matter, really, since I could find my way out of those familiar woods blindfolded, but again, I didn't want to spook the deer so close to the season opener. Walking too quickly again, I made myself stop and try to absorb the slower rhythms of the woods. It worked—not well, but it worked. When my breathing slowed again and my pulse no longer pounded in my temple, I raised my boot to move on. A twig snapping in the woods to my left caused my foot to hang in midair, and I stood there like that, in suspended animation, for a long time. I peered intently into the saplings where the sound had come from, but the undergrowth was still too green, the forest still hiding many of its mysteries under its summer clothing. I couldn't see a thing. Crouching once again, I waited five minutes. The wind had died. The place was dead quiet, save for the few birds fluttering around the treetops. But the sound didn't repeat itself.

I knew it was a deer.

Moving on, I stepped carefully through the last stand of oaks and into the logging road where the ATV was parked. I didn't come out exactly where I'd intended, but the place was familiar. I had missed the machine by eighty yards. Turning left, I walked up the road and around the final corner. It had been almost pitch black in the woods, but out in the open I lifted my hand to shield my eyes from the surprisingly bright clouds illuminated from beneath by a sun that had set only moments ago. It only took a second to spot the machine, a disruption of the neat, linear saplings at the edge of the woods.

But something was out of place.

I could see the front tire of the old three-wheeler, but from that distance it appeared to have the hindquarter of a large deer protruding from it. Slinging my rifle onto my shoulder, I used both hands to cup my eyes and verify that there was indeed a deer standing next to the ATV. Smiling to myself, I trod quietly up the trail toward the deer and my ride home. Whether it saw me or not I don't know, but it continued on past the machine and dissolved into the thick tangle of saplings beyond. I scanned the woods for any sign of antlers—it was big enough in body to have been the eight-pointer—but the creature was long gone.

Amid the glorious silence of the encroaching evening, a snort behind me caused me to involuntarily jump and bang my knee on the side of the Honda. Turning slowly, I saw a large doe peering at me from the other side of the woods. Behind her, two fawns. The fawns began moving daintily back into the cover of the woods as the doe remained focused, her large ears like radar dishes aimed precisely at me. She bobbed her head once, then again. I let out a low fawn call, thinking I sounded remarkably like a whitetail. The doe promptly raced off into the woods in abject terror.

Sitting for a moment on the machine, I listened to the woods calming back down after the deer's crashing departure. But night was falling rapidly, and it was past time to go. On the way out, I begrudged the soft whine of the old motor for depriving me of the sounds of the dying summer. Halfway across the large, sapling-studded field leading to my house, I longed for one last listen. So I let the machine coast to a stop and turned off the key.

The sky was alive with strange twittering cries, and within moments a half-dozen woodcock flew over my head, dropping in from points north, I imagined. Closing my eyes, I envisioned the dogs working these same fields only two short weeks from now. I imagined the doe and the fawns feeding past my tree stand, perhaps leading the buck to me. Perhaps not.

I tend not to work as hard for the deer once pheasant season has opened.

A shrill peeping caused me to jerk my head around. A very large woodcock was headed straight for me, nearly at eye level. His large, black eye, full of the reflection of the dying sun, met mine for an instant before he broke off, spooked by my presence.

The cool air carried to me the faint peeps of tree frogs, still trying to hang onto the last remnants of summer; I smiled, knowing it was already gone.

The Preserve

Every year or two, depending on funds that are usually quite undependable, when the dogs and I can no longer stand the wait for bird season and the final February rabbit hunt is little more than a cold memory, I treat us all to a preserve hunt. It usually takes place in September, the earliest month the law permits you to hunt "set" birds in New York. Last year, it was probably a little too warm to run the dogs, but they didn't seem to mind at all. In fact, despite the heat,

Author accepting a pheasant from Ted.

the intolerable wait caused those beasts to virtually explode from the back of the truck in ecstasy when they realized where we were.

My father, who had never killed a pheasant during his many trips afield with me (or in his entire life, for that matter), ridiculed me each time I returned home from hunting birds that only hours before had been released from cages transported atop the handlebars of an ATV. I will not itemize his list of criticisms, but let it stand that the words "zoo" and "chicken" cropped up quite frequently.

My own thoughts on shooting preserves have evolved (or *devolved*, as Dad would undoubtedly say) to the point at which I enjoy a great deal of satisfaction and excitement during an afternoon of chasing pen-raised pheasants and the occasional quail or chukar. Despite the relative assurance of seeing some game, the hunts are not guaranteed. The preserve I annually hunt is an expanse of western New York that looks much like the rest of it did during those wonderful, mysterious years when birds were plentiful. There are no fences, just a huge plot of old farmland. Vast fields of wild sawgrass, a rarity anywhere else in the county now, reach from horizon to horizon, tugging at your legs with toothy blades. Near the ground the sawgrass creates matted corridors of vegetation and millions of hiding places for the stocked birds and wilder wildlife. I don't doubt the place supports a decent population of native ringnecks. The fields are surrounded on all sides by dense shelterbelts and hedgerows and are split down the middle by a large creek, which flows powerfully after a good rain. The creek bottom is a favorite haunt for the birds that escape the gunners and their dogs. This place is wild looking and wonderful and will wear you to the bone with its knolls and hills, and by the day's end you almost forget the artificial origins of the birds. But my father continued to claim otherwise, playing familiar refrains about tame birds and easy shots. It bothered me, so I did the meanest thing I could think of: I invited him to come along.

The owner thought us fairly out of our heads to run the dogs with the temperatures nearing 80 degrees, but he had an area well suited to a hot-day hunt, if we still wanted to try it. On one end of the field is a large irrigation pond and at the other a smaller one. Along the edge, the creek runs cool and clear all summer and fall. After each pass through the area, the dogs can swim and drink to their hearts' content. I could see the look on my dad's face as we signed in and paid our money: *This is really roughing it, kid.*

Having been here a few times before, I'd often heard the owner's familiar line about how "the last bunch of guys missed a whole mess of birds, so once I stock, the field should be loaded." His predictability didn't disappoint me. He told us to wait twenty minutes before heading into the field, as always. This time, however, I became suspicious when I never saw him head for the hunting area with the bird crates on his old ATV. Frankly, I wondered if we were being cheated. I tried to dismiss the thought, knowing there well *could* have been a bunch of guys, as the owner insisted, who paid for twenty birds and didn't shoot more than three and so the field was still crawling with the survivors. I just doubted it. We had, after all, paid for only ten birds, and if the survivors in the field were anywhere near the number the owner claimed, he shouldn't have to stock anymore. But after shelling out several hours' pay apiece, my friend Brian, Dad, and I were not easy to convince.

I have to admit that I've had only one bad hunt at the preserve over the years, and that was due to a friend's golden retriever that would not hunt for us at all that day. That left poor Ted to hunt for three of us on a blistering hot day, and we were nowhere near the stream. It took several cooling-breaks and hard brush busting to get only half of the birds we paid for.

That was then. This was now. I'd never had a hunt end poorly due to negligence of the owner of the place, so I tried to generate some enthusiasm. We were finally, after that interminable wait and despite the admittedly artificial conditions, hunting pheasants.

Knowing these stocked birds could be fairly wily and run the dogs nearly as far and as fast as any wild ringneck, I approached the field with a calm air of smugness, figuring on giving my dad a real hunt and silencing his preserve–hunt pestering forever. Dad approached it with a thin smile that I didn't like at all.

"Don't be afraid to shoot when they come up. They'll get out on you quick," I said.

Right about then, Maggie flushed the first hen, which in its suicidal flight nearly took Brian's hat off, just cleared me, and then banked around my father and out into the field.

I shot it before Dad could comment, but that didn't stop him.

"Seems a shame to shoot it when you could have just reached up and grabbed it."

Thankfully, the rest of the afternoon proved a bit more challenging, especially for my father. The ringnecks gave us some hair-raising down-field runs and wild flushes that would have made a wild rooster proud. Brian and I shot exceptionally well (that is to say, compared to our normal exceptionally *poor* shooting), and we had eight of ten birds in our game bags before we realized my dad still hadn't shot his first.

"You know," Dad began, "I really want to get my first bird, so on the next flush, slow down a little. You guys are killing these things before I even get my safety off!"

We snickered behind his back as he turned to follow Ted, who was suddenly interested in something near the base of an enormous, round hay bale.

"Ted's hot," I said to no one in particular.

"You two just stay cool," Dad said to Brian and me.

I have to give my father credit; his gun came up quickly as the hen pheasant launched into the air just above Ted's nose. He shot quickly, too, but none of his three shots even clipped a tail feather before the bird beat it resolutely for the security of the creek bottom.

"What now?" Dad asked, his patience gone.

"I'll take Teddy and find it. You guys keep hunting."

Brian and Dad hunted over Maggie while I took Ted and began walking downhill. Ted had just disappeared over the stone fence separating the creek from the field when I heard a leathery flapping of wings and breaking of branches. I leaped onto the stone fence to watch Ted chasing the hen through some brambles. When it burst from cover over the fence forty yards away, I waited until it was safely away from Ted's nose before dropping it as it rose. I saw my father's and Brian's heads snap around at the shot. Ted retrieved the bird from the edge of the creek, dropped it at my feet, and then returned to the water, lying down in it and smiling up at me.

Out in the field, I could plainly see Dad was not smiling.

Stuffing the hen into my vest, I started back across the field. Before I had even closed half of the hundred yards back to my hunting partners, I heard the startled squawks of two roosters flushed by Maggie from some heavy cover. A volley of shots followed, and I noticed Brian didn't shoot until my dad's gun was empty. By then the birds were out of range and sailed up the field untouched. Good thing, since we had paid for only one more bird and I didn't want my dad to go home without getting his.

Believe me when I say I did *not* want that to happen.

At some point as I crossed the field, Ted got birdy again, and I happened to look at the action of my autoloader. The last shell—the one that had dropped the hen—protruded at an unnatural angle from the action, and I sighed at my gun's penchant for jamming at inopportune times. Sticking my thumb in to clear the jam, as I had hundreds of times before, I kept one eye on Brian and my father. The shell cleared and the action slammed home—on my thumb. Dancing prettily around the field in delicate circles and

Maggie with a hen pheasant.

graceful loops with my hitchhiking digit still lodged in the heart of the Mossberg, I was in unmitigated agony.

My father's 20-gauge popped again as he and Brian, oblivious to my dilemma, continued on up the field. Ted looked quizzically back at me, charging slightly forward at the shot, then back at me again.

"Go ahead. Don't worry about me."

Ted raced upfield to join Maggie in the sudden flurry of action. We may have been fairly inept hunters, but the guys before us had to have been absolutely *hopeless.* The field was full of birds.

Unfortunately, Dad still hadn't hit one.

Dislodging my thumb by yanking back on the lever, I stifled a pained yelp as blood spurted up my shirt from my bisected thumbnail. Wrapping it in a tissue, I carefully reloaded the carnivorous Mossberg with my good left hand—if you think *that* was easy, try it sometime—and moved on to join the party.

If it is possible for a human being's eyes to burn red, it was happening to my father. He had missed four birds straight. Behind him, Brian shrugged. The atmosphere was thick enough without me dwelling on my injury—other than asking them to stop once while I opened my nail to relieve the pressure that was building to incredible heights.

Finally, my father said, "Next one that comes up, you guys take it. I'm done."

I felt bad, but Brian and I both agreed. Fortunately, the next one that came up flashed only briefly across in front of us before disappearing into the thick oak woods along the north side of the field. With my damaged hand, I had no intention of shooting, and my body effectively blocked Brian from a shot. My father seemed completely disinterested.

"Not as easy as you thought?" I couldn't resist asking my father—perhaps the blood loss had made me delirious.

He answered with an eloquent glare.

Just then, a rooster lifted off inches in front of Maggie and only ten yards from Dad. His gun came up and the bird crumpled in an angry burst of feathers.

"If I can get one," my father said, once again smiling his thin smile, "how hard can it be?"

Case Closed

With only a short time until pheasant season, I was bursting with energy and didn't mind the long walk. Actually, I was pleased that the farmer who owned the land had finally wised up and put concrete barriers across the lane leading to the back of the property. It would make things more difficult for the dozens of guys who didn't have permission to gain access to the grass and cornfields, the woodlot, and the duck ponds. For years the place had been a playground for all types of hunters, most of whom just assumed it was OK to hunt the property. The farmer, one of the few left in the county who didn't heavily post his land with No Trespassing signs, didn't seem to mind the hunters. A couple of years ago, though, he did complain about the kids on their ATVs flattening some of his rows of corn while making shortcuts around the fields. That's why the barriers went up.

I used to be able to drive all the way back to the pheasant field, but on the way I hopscotched over a lot of thick blackberry tangles and dense dogwood thickets—great pheasant cover. Now, with the vehicle barriers, we would be walking the whole way every time. Maggie didn't seem to mind, bouncing in and out of the thick undergrowth, glancing back now and then to see if I was still with her.

With rabbit season open, I was carrying the beat-up old Stoeger side-by-side, but I didn't really care if we saw any cottontails. My mission was to make one last inspection of the land—a place we've found to be a holdout for wild pheasants—before bird season. Theoretically, anyway, if not emotionally, I could have just driven there on the opener and let the dogs go to town, but I had to see. I had to *know*. This land and this farmer had surprised me—rarely pleasantly—in the past.

Several years earlier, I'd planned to hunt geese on the large pond in the center of the property, only to find that the trees around the pond had been bulldozed in and the creek feeding it diverted into a new drainage ditch. What was once a wonderful two-acre habitat for waterfowl and deer had been turned, nearly overnight, into a muddy pothole. I am still not quite sure why it was done—the move seemed to serve no purpose other than to displace some wildlife. Similarly, just a couple of years earlier, the adjoining woodlot had been logged off. Where I once hunted deer and squirrels and raccoons, the heart of the woods, great stands of hickory and oak and beech, had been logged out with all the surgical precision of a jackknife amputation. Now the center of the woods was so choked with brambles and berry bushes that it was nearly impossible to walk through them. And, mysteriously, several of the mammoth hardwoods still lay where they were felled, as if the logging company had gone belly-up halfway through the demolition of the woods and no one had ever bothered to come back and finish up.

Good dogs!

So now, in rabbit season, I was apprehensive as I walked up the lane, an old railway that had long ago been stripped of its tracks. Most of the property was now jammed with crops—not that I blamed the farmer for that, since farming is his business, after all—but one small and relatively hidden corner had provided us several wild ringnecks over the years. It was a small wedge of what appeared to be wild switchgrass, jammed between the crop fields and the old railway and surrounded on three sides by high walls of thorns. The field gave the birds cover and food and—perhaps most important—was more than a mile from the road. I'd seen pheasant hunters on other parts of the property, but never here. Now, with the concrete barrier up back at the road, I was willing to bet we'd never see another hunter here.

Turning left off the lane and onto a tractor path down through the tall stalks, I heard Maggie huffing and snorting back in the corn. Something moved in my peripheral vision, and I whirled to my right as a large cottontail rabbit emerged with Maggie just behind it. I pointed the shotgun at it, but Maggie was so close that I didn't dare shoot. Bird dog and prey disappeared into the corn on the opposite side of the tractor path. A few moments passed before Maggie returned to my side, panting, her short tail wagging at an incredible speed.

At a barely discernible dip in the path, we turned right into the tall corn. Maggie raced ahead of me, remembering precisely where we were going. Tall, brittle stalks brushed my shoulders. A few moments passed before the corn rows began to make a slight bend. I paused, not wanting to go farther into the corn if I was headed in the wrong direction. These fields could be—and usually were—virtually endless. More than once I'd emerged after chasing the dogs— which were in turn chasing a pheasant—at a clearing or a tractor path with the realization and resulting trepidation that I didn't have the slightest clue where I was. Today, I was on a specific mission, and that was to check out the pheasant field and be home by supper. I had no desire to be lost in the stalks. Listening for Maggie, I realized that she was no longer anywhere near me. The familiar *whish-whish* her dainty legs made running through the corn was notably absent. But before hitting the dog whistle in a panic, I let the cornrows take me around just one more slight bend, where I could see light at the end of the rows. I was thankful when I emerged, but that thankfulness went away with the speed of a flushing rooster.

Only forty yards from me, Maggie was sniffing at a small clump of weeds, up to her knees in the muck of what was left of the switchgrass field. It was gone. Plowed under. Destroyed. Turning back into the corn and whistling for Maggie, I did not wallow in the vision.

I was disappointed, but not surprised. I thought immediately of the pond and the woods. The place had a sad, irrefutable history of abuse when it came to habitat preservation. There was no reason to hope or believe that this perfectly good, black-dirt field would be left for the game animals. None whatsoever. The grass field had been inexplicably plowed in October and not planted with winter rye or anything else, and I was instantly reminded of the recklessly logged trees in the woodlot, now in an advanced state of decomposition. There was just no rhyme or reason. It seemed a waste, in the most literal definition of the word.

Sulking back through the corn, I made a mental list of the places we had available to hunt wild birds this year. There was Betty's field, JK's out in Somerset, the field in Cambria; of course, there was always Ransomville (although I had long ago learned not to say *always* about any of these places) and the place in Wilson. Following the accounting of that dismal, short list, I made the mistake of mentally inventorying the places we'd lost in just the past five years.

Sadly, that list was much longer.

I sighed to myself. *There's always the club,* I guessed. But I had no wish to spend a single day of the wild-pheasant season chasing stocked birds around the club. It was not in my plans. This place had been good to us, and in return we hadn't abused it, being very careful not to overhunt it. Last year I killed one bird here and saw several others flushing wild in the distance. Maggie put the bird out of the corn and chased it down through the sumacs on the north side. Three times I'd caught glimpses of the big rooster as it ducked in and out of the corn, in and out of the hedgerow, in and out of the lane. When it headed out into the long, tangled grass of the field, I lost track of Maggie and was certain I had lost any chance at the pheasant—not uncommon with these wild ones. When I spotted my dog, I thought she had turned back to me in apparent defeat. But unknown to me and Maggie, the rooster was pinned between us and had no choice but to flush as Maggie closed the wedge as she returned to my side. I can still see that bird hanging in midair, cackling madly, Maggie jumping up beneath it, the golden field waiting to catch the rooster downed by a shot I don't even remember making. We flushed another bird shortly thereafter, but I didn't shoot it, feeling that I had taken my fair share. After that, I retired the place for the year.

Stalking back up the trail, I knew we would come back here. We'd hunt the corn around the pond, and the couple of drainage ditches that would still hold the odd bird or two. But without the little golden field, something would be missing. Another piece of our history—Maggie's and mine—buried beneath the good black dirt that will next year undoubtedly sprout with something mundane like corn or beans, perfectly assimilated into the monotonous sea of crop fields, never to be seen again as prime bird habitat.

Everyone has his or her priorities, but measuring a crop field against the protection of some badly needed wildlife habitat seemed a poor trade-off to me. You can plant beans and corn year after year—they will always grow. On the other hand, the vast majority of the pheasant population has been gone since the 1970s. This admittedly small scar on the land was just one more nail in the coffin of the birds' recovery. A few more nails and it won't matter anymore.

The case will be closed for good.

CHAPTER TWO

THE WARMUP

Opening Day of Woodcock Season

It was pouring. Greta, with her long hair bound in a ponytail and wearing my old Filson coat, looked understandably unhappy. Already soaked to my waist, I wasn't terribly pleased, either, but I have come to expect that opening day—*any* opening day—is not likely to greet me with fair weather and crisp blue skies. Blue-sky days come, but not usually right away. It seems you have to earn those by wading through a half-dozen or so of these.

At this rate, we would be owed a month of blue sky.

Maggie and Ted were happily bounding around, their wet coats and the cold temperature giving them added incentive to keep moving, and fast. I'm not sure if they knew we were after woodcock or not, but I decided to run them around the pheasant fields for a while before fighting our way back into the woodcock thicket. I suspect that if Greta had known that we were standing out in the rain scouting for pheasants instead of heading directly for our intended targets, she may have shot me. If she did realize it, she didn't say anything—and she didn't shoot me.

The place, not far from my house, just never seems to hold pheasants. Oh, there is cover for them, and corn across the road, but over the past several years I can count the pheasants I have seen there on two fingers. Quite a few acres of short grass near the road give way to longer grass interspersed with clumps of dogwood. Beyond that, the grass peters out, and there is nothing but a nasty, dense thicket of dogwood and blackberry and beech saplings. That's where the woodcock live. It is not one of the visual gems of Niagara County, but it is always good for a woodcock or two and sometimes many more, if not a pheasant. As we circled the front field twice, the rain flogged us even harder.

Giving up on the pheasants after forty-five minutes of not seeing a thing, we headed back through the transitional grass and dogwoods and were suddenly, not even halfway back to the thicket, into woodcock. The first bird twittered into the air from a tiny clump

Woodcock hiding in the leaves.

of dogwood. Greta and I both shot as it flew broadside at about twenty yards. The bird sailed untouched back toward the road. We followed it back to the small patch of ash saplings where it had landed. Mysteriously, the dogs never picked up its scent again, and we never saw it flush. Maybe it walked across the road.

Hunting woodcock with flushing dogs is a game of reflexes and dog watching. Pointers, the preferred and much more logical selection of dog for timberdoodles and grouse, will lock up and point the tiny birds, giving the gunners an opportunity to prepare for a shot. Ted and Maggie, on the other hand, dash invisibly through the thick, nasty brush and flush birds, running them down as soon as they smell them. You can't blame them, really, since they are accustomed to pheasants, which will run away if you give them the chance. When you work flushing dogs for pheasants, there is generally a small amount of time between the dogs' first contact with game and the flush, giving you a moment of preparation for the shot. With woodcock, there rarely is. Oh, every now and then I will catch a glimpse of Ted making a hard 90-degree turn as he smells a woodcock and prepares to pounce, but more often than not, a bird is suddenly in the air.

Unlike pheasants, which take a moment or two to gain speed, woodcock flush as if cable-launched off an aircraft carrier. By the time you see them, they are flying *fast*. And when you finally get your gun up, they will have put several trees between you and themselves. Often, by the time you have your safety off and are preparing to shoot, they are already back on the ground, usually forty or fifty yards away. For birds that migrate thousands of miles in the fall, they certainly don't like to fly far. For those who hunt over flushing dogs, the woodcock's tendency for short flights is their one saving grace. Once a woodcock is flushed and missed or not shot at, you at least have an idea where it went. Then you can prepare, sending the dogs back in for the flush. We kill more timberdoodles on the second, third, and fourth flushes than we do on all the original flushes combined.

Before Greta and I even reached the thicket, we had flushed seven woodcock out of the relatively open cover of the dogwood fields. I was surprised to find the birds lurking in many places we'd never flushed them before, attributing it to the heavy rain and dark gray day. They probably feel more comfortable out in the open on murky days than they do on the more traditional bright-blue October days. That was fine with me.

Of those first seven flushes by five different birds, we killed . . . *ahem* . . . *one.* An unlucky bird that had evaded two deafening volleys finally flew out the wrong end of a small brushy clump and across the end of my gun. Feeling a bit sporting, I let the bird get out several yards before dropping him. Sadly, we had missed so many shots that the dogs did not even come looking for the retrieve after my latest blast.

"Fetch it up!" I yelled.

Ted and Maggie both appeared at Greta's side, peeking out from the clump where they'd flushed the bird for the second time. Remaining still and staring at me, they looked doubtful.

"Fetch it up. *Really!*"

Maggie trotted into the field with her nub wagging and pounced on the dead bird as if expecting it to fly away again. She brought it and dropped it at my feet, not waiting for praise before disappearing back into the ever-thickening cover.

Once inside the confines of the actual thicket, we had to duck and back our way through a variety of nasty thorns before reaching some semblance of an opening. Letting the dogs work around us in a circle, we managed to miss three more woodcock, not exactly imbuing the dogs with any faith in our shooting. Ted did come back to check on whether we hit one—but only the *first* time. An hour passed in the covert with only a handful of shots, far fewer than we'd had out in the more open areas, so we elected to fight our way back out and work around a small duck pond, giving the dogs a chance to take a break and get a drink as well. At the edge of the pond, two more woodcock went up. I shamefully missed one of them—a depressingly easy shot—while Greta swore she hit the other. When we sent the dogs in to fetch the dead bird, we *both* missed it as it flushed again. Woodcock have the unnerving tendency to fold up as if shot, when in fact they have not been touched. It's all part of the erratic style of flight that makes them so hard to hit. At times they don't so much land as *fling* themselves at the ground. Tricky devils, but I guess if someone was shooting at me, I, too, would be flinging myself at the ground.

Discovering that our shared box of shells had dwindled to six—yes, that's right—we decided to head back toward the road, debating on the way whether to restock our vests with shells at the truck or wring out our clothes and head home. Greta was about ready to go. I was disappointed, wanting her to get her first woodcock. She looked less interested in that prospect than in getting home and into some dry clothes. Reluctantly admitting that we probably should stop for the day, we had just turned back for the road when another woodcock erupted off the tip of Maggie's nose from under a small bush in a fairly open spot. Greta shot it with quickness that bordered on vengeance, smiling as Ted picked the bird up by a wingtip and carried it to me.

"Let's get out of here," she said.

On the way out, we flushed two more and heard two others go off on the opposite side of a hedgerow that Ted was working. We arrived at the truck with two more woodcock than we had come in with.

And twenty-one fewer shells.

Hunt-club Opener

This year I joined a pheasant-hunting club. With the numbers of wild birds dwindling, I've begun feeling steadily more guilty each time I remove a wild rooster from one of that last handful of places I hold so near to my heart. So, with the shooting club I belong to offering a limited hunting program, I decided to sign up. Starting a couple of weeks before the wild-bird season, the club releases birds each weekend, and the season is open much longer than the four-week wild-bird season. Choosing to become a member of the club wasn't so much a matter of wanting to shoot birds earlier in the fall and for more weeks every year as it was to spare the wild-bird population while still giving Maggie and Ted the work they need and crave. I'm not much of a joiner—never have been—but a friend of mine got me into the club and was going to join the hunt program with me. Of course, at the last minute he declined, feeling that his setter pup was still too young to warrant the several-hundred-dollar investment. So that left me, Mr. Outgoing, with a bunch of strangers on the club's pheasant-hunting opener.

We met at the clubhouse first thing in the morning. Most of the men were in small groups, talking among themselves. When Ted and I walked in, several heads turned to look, not so much at me as at the dog, as if to say, "What the hell is he?" Ted, I am convinced, is mostly Labrador, probably from English bloodlines, but he bears little resemblance to the long-coated, pointy-nosed, tall Labs that the guys in the club were accustomed to seeing. Ted has a large black block for a head, very short legs, and a fairly wiry yet sleek and oily coat. At five years old, he has the temperament and energy of a six-month-old puppy. I elected to bring him instead of Maggie because he isn't rangy and was much less likely to run over to someone else's hunting area—a big fear of mine in this band of strangers on our debut day.

In the clubhouse, dogs lounged everywhere. Mostly old, fat springers (for a fleeting moment, I wished I'd brought Maggie), they lay like fuzzy, bloated floor mats at the feet of their gossiping, coffee-drinking masters. Finding the coffeepot, I looped Ted's leash through the back of my chair and sat down to read the paper. I figured the paper would keep me from just sitting there looking stupid if no one decided to talk to me. But as so often happens in the company of dog people, Ted broke the ice for me. One by one, most of the other guys filed by, petting Ted (and undoubtedly pondering his origins) and eventually introducing themselves to me.

I wasn't reading the paper for long.

With the room brimming now with about fifteen men and seven or eight dogs, we drew numbers for starting points. At these specific places in the pheasant fields at precisely 7:30, we could unleash the eager animals. The agreement was to hunt in our areas for about twenty minutes, and thereafter to feel free to roam about the place, of course following the rules of gentlemanly bird hunting. (I didn't really know any of those rules, so I decided early on to stay far away from everyone else as long as I could.) Thankfully, by the following weekend the drawing system was abandoned when it was generally assumed that no one was ungentlemanly. (Considering that I was the only new member of the club, I wondered later if the test had been tailored for me.)

It felt good to be back outside, away from the smoke and the constant battle with the stubborn force at the opposite end of the leash that wanted to sniff every pretty little springer that walked by. Ted was much calmer outside.

The Channel Four weatherman out of Buffalo, Chuck Gurney, had just the previous day signed off for the last time before moving on to Cleveland. (Could Buffalo possibly be worse than *Cleveland*?) I can't help thinking that his final forecast was a joke, a farewell gag. He called for sleet and wind and freezing rain. When I set foot on the clubhouse deck with the sun rising through the far hedgerow, the sky was a cool, brittle blue with a band of subtle pink, and there wasn't even a hint of a breeze. I hadn't brought my camera, because it was supposed to be miserable, and now it looked like one of the most photogenic days I had seen so far this year: Orange-clad men and their dogs were everywhere. The fields were touched by a ghostly hint of frost. The sky's blue was deepening by the moment, and the fields were full of birds. I could hear them already. And I didn't have my camera.

Thanks, Chuck. I hope Cleveland *is nice.*

We set out across the fields, and Ted began straining at the leash again. I noticed several other dogs being unleashed but kept old Blockhead tethered for another moment or two—a wise decision.

As the men began disappearing up various trails through the woods and brush toward some of the farther fields, the hunter immediately to my right, perhaps a hundred yards away but screened by brush, began yelling "*whoa . . . whoa!*" Ted locked in on the sound and homed in even more intensely on that location when the other hunter's shotgun erupted three times in quick succession. Clearing the brushy hedgerow separating us, a pheasant locked its wings, soaring into the switchgrass field a hundred yards farther out. Ted marked the bird and whined like a puppy, eager to go after it. I was thankful I had him on the leash and could just picture the ugliness that might have ensued when the other hunter burst through the hedgerow just in time to see his bird departing for points unknown. Ted strained even

Ted with a face full of rooster pheasant.

harder, not comprehending why we weren't racing ninety miles an hour down the field after this bird like we usually do, pulling hard enough to cut off the circulation in my hand. I let ten minutes pass on the watch attached to my numb wrist before walking Ted around the corner of the hedgerow. The other hunter was a rapidly fading orange dot in the huge field to the north. Apparently, he did not think the big rooster worth going after.

Fine with me and Ted.

With the dog still leashed, I slowly walked toward the pheasant's likely touchdown spot and stopped just short of it. Sitting stoically, finally tired of choking against the strain of his leash, Ted was in the middle of perhaps his four-hundredth heavy sigh when I loaded my shotgun. I bent over, and at the sound of the leash clip opening, he was gone, covering the thirty yards like a dart thrown into a bull's-eye by a strong man. The rooster must have walked when it hit the ground. I wasn't surprised. Ted pounced up and down, shifted directions twenty times in ten seconds, and finally the first bird of the year was in the air. The shot, unlike many harder ones undoubtedly to follow in the coming months, was easy. The bird towered straight up, hanging in the air in a moment of indecision about which way to fly. Once he made up his mind, I let him get out several yards before shooting with a calm air of confidence. The second shot was not so confident. The third, a hastily applied Hail Mary, took him down, and I looked quickly around to see if anyone had seen the pathetic display of wingshooting. I knew they'd heard it, but at least no one got to witness it, so I could never be forced to swear it was my shot. Ted retrieved the bird with his usual enthusiasm.

Working my way toward a thicker section of the property, I heard several volleys of shots that sounded even more dismal than mine, these apparently issuing from not one but two poor wingshooters. *Bang bang bang. Bang-ba-ba-bang,* followed by no calls for a retrieve or shouts of triumph. I couldn't help smiling.

Halfway down a bush-hogged trail through some beech saplings, Ted began acting birdy, quartering this way and that in jerky motions and finally diving into the thick saplings. He began racing parallel to the trail, barely visible in the thick gray trees. Forty-five yards ahead of us, a hen beat wings to clear the ground, and I dropped her just before she would have vanished.

At the club, both hens and roosters are legal (with wild birds, only cocks can be taken). The other freedom lacking in wild-bird hunting is that at a club there are no limits on the number of pheasants you may shoot. Up until now, the word "limit" simply wasn't pertinent to my pheasant hunting. In New York, the limit on pheasants is two, and the very few times my hunting partners and I limited out were causes for major celebration. But now I understand the importance of limits and the propensity for overconsumption in their absence. In less than an hour of hunting, we had two birds. Granted, they were not very *wild* birds, but they were ringnecks nonetheless. At the original club meeting, we'd been advised not to be game hogs, but we were never given a specific number of birds we could or should shoot in any given time period. I elected to quit at two.

I had not yet leashed Ted, who was even more full of energy with two successes under our belt, but I unloaded my gun and began a long, wide swing back toward the clubhouse. I wanted to explore some of the property I had not yet seen and watch some of the other hunters from a courteous distance. None of them, it seemed, was getting even remotely off the beaten track. The club practices a "soft" release, in which birds are set out the day before to get acclimated to the area before they're hunted. This seems fairly sporting, but it also means that they wander and fly around, not sticking to the easy places where they were dropped off. Some semblance of natural instinct takes over and tells them—at least the ones that survive the coyotes and foxes for a night or two—to hide. I naturally started hunting the thicker spots, while the majority of the guys were running their dogs in wide-open, sparse grass. Although I witnessed a couple of shots, the guys in the open fields were not enjoying a lot of success.

In a dogwood thicket on the way back to the clubhouse, we flushed two more birds, one a fine rooster, which I am sure I would have been tempted to shoot had my gun been loaded. Ted was a bit disturbed by my lack of interest in killing the bird and promptly decided to run after it. Shortly after that, I leashed him for the rest of the several-hundred-yard walk back to the clubhouse, but I have no doubt that he would have flushed more birds if he'd been allowed to hunt. I was in heaven. And I did that well with *Ted*, the overgrown puppy, for crying out loud. What would Maggie do in a place like this? I couldn't wait to find out.

It was nearly 9:30. Nearly? It was *only* 9:30. The only other time I killed birds that fast was at the preserve. I knew I was going to like this place. Sipping another cup of terribly strong coffee, I sat on the back deck of the clubhouse watching two hunters working their springers in the nearby field. I started hunting pheasants without any other pheasant hunters around to guide me, much less teach me how to dog-handle, so it was fun to watch and listen to other guys saying and doing the same things I do.

"Get *in there!*" one of the orange coats would yell, his voice carrying on the morning breeze.

"Get *back* here!" the other one would fruitlessly yell at the bouncing brown-and-white blur out in front of him.

I am not alone—there are others of my kind, I thought, smiling to myself.

The first few hunters began trickling in about forty minutes later, and only two had pheasants. The fifteen men hunting had taken only five birds, and Ted and I had two of them. The hunters' comments ranged from "What a beautiful morning to be out there" to "I don't think there's a live bird in the county." When the other guys saw the two pheasants Ted was guarding (when he wasn't trying to mount one of their springers), the nods and other unspoken language seemed to range from *Nice job* to *What a jerk,* plus several nondescript grunts that may have indicated the former while truly believing the latter.

It didn't take me long to figure out who in the club I would eventually befriend. The guys who did sit to drink coffee and shoot the breeze with me were intrigued by Ted, the blockhead, now that they realized he could hunt.

I couldn't wait for them to meet Maggie.

Looking for Woodcock

This time, I couldn't scout for pheasants. We were woodcock hunting, period. After a couple years of being invited, Greta's dad, Howard, finally showed up to watch us bird hunt. An avid deer hunter, he had never gone wingshooting with us in all these years, and I was pleased that at least some birds were around to show him. I was hoping that watching us would inspire him to come up and join us for the real highlight of the year, pheasant season.

That Saturday morning was the flip side of the conditions Greta and I had suffered through a day earlier. Gray skies gave way to deep, cerulean blue. The moon hung on into daylight, a pale globe just above the far dogwood thicket. The air was crisp, and a hint of northern breeze had already shucked off the thin husk of early morning fog. The ground was surprisingly firm after yesterday's late-day downpour, but the underbrush was still wet. The nippiness of the air combined with instantly wet clothing gave us a chill, but we would be sweating before long.

I dropped the tailgate, and in seconds Maggie and Ted disappeared into the wet cover. Before we were even out of sight of the road, a cottontail raced up the trail ahead of us, and I removed a large clump of dirt inches behind its rump. The dogs, still excited, briefly returned to us to see if any fetching duties were required before quickly melting back into the brush, their location revealed to us only by the tinkling of the tags on their collars and the occasional snapping branch.

I've always done well on damp mornings, so I held my shotgun at the ready, as did Greta, anticipating action like we'd had last time. I prayed I'd shoot better today. Howard brought up the rear, watching the dogs. He'd known them merely as house dogs that jump on him when he comes to visit, but he was visibly impressed with their lack of goofiness when they had a job to do. We worked several small clumps of dogwood where we'd flushed birds before but didn't find a creature beneath their burgundy branches. I wasn't worried, though, knowing we would do well back in the more traditional timberdoodle cover in the thicket.

"Deer!" Howard said, pointing out to the side I hadn't been watching, my concentration focused entirely on the dogs. Greta didn't see it either, and thankfully the dogs did not show any interest. They rarely chase deer, and then only reflexively for a short distance. Maggie had a puppyhood encounter with a six-point buck that left her with respect for the local whitetails. We were rabbit hunting her first winter when she spotted a buck bedded in a hedgerow behind my house and ran up to it, woofing and growling. The buck simply stood and lowered its spindly little rack to within a foot of her and made a false charge, stamping its foot. She's never messed much with deer since.

Greta dropped in behind me, talking on and off with her father. As we neared the thicket, I clearly heard him say, "Where the hell are we going now?" I bent over and headed up one of the deer trails into the center of the thicket, branches whipping at the exposed skin of my face and neck. Once into the relatively open eye of the brushy storm of branches, I turned around to watch the slower progress of my wife and Howard. The dogs were already circling the thicket, and I was sure I'd be shooting at any moment.

"Is this where we're going to see some birds?" Howard asked, straightening his back after dislodging a branch from his sweatshirt.

"Yep."

Of course, we didn't. Without fail, when you are trying to show off something you enjoy to someone, it just won't work. It happens with fishing, especially during the steelhead run. I'll have an eight-fish night and invite someone to come back with me the next day, and there will not be a fish in sight. It happens with deer hunting. And it happens a *lot* in bird hunting.

Maggie with a mouthful of timberdoodle.

We worked our way slowly through the no-fail thicket and didn't flush a single woodcock. I tried to remember a previous total skunking but couldn't. Finally, when Greta and Howard looked as if they had tired of the unproductive, claustrophobic confines of the brush, we turned back.

Buried in the center of the thicket are a few old cars, trees now growing up through them. Around the north edge of this tiny wilderness junkyard is a dense thorn patch that the dogs hate but the woodcock love. Just as I heard the metallic clunking of Ted walking across the detached hood of a 1969 Olds, a woodcock went up to the right, peeping invisibly.

"There's one," I said glumly.

"Where?" Howard asked.

"It flew off through the woods," Greta said glumly.

Howard gave a subtle nod, not at all convincing me that he believed us.

Deciding to work the dogs in the tight cover surrounding the pond, I was beginning to fret. Howard had never even *seen* a woodcock, and I really wanted to get a couple. Last year, I discovered a tight little path through two straight rows of dense brush that I came to call the Tunnel. The Tunnel, like the thicket, was always good for a bird or two. Then again, the thicket wasn't any good today, so who knew what might happen in the Tunnel. But after fruitlessly following the dogs through the thick brush at the pond, I headed there anyway.

Howard followed me into the brushy corridor while Greta paralleled us along the outside. This was a killer tactic. The birds nearly always flew out to the left. With Greta out there, she'd have a good chance for a shot. I can't remember ever *not* flushing a bird here.

Maggie and Ted, slowing in the increasing heat of the morning, excitedly dove in ahead of us, perhaps also remembering all our past successes here. Perhaps? Oh, they remember, all right. With the dogs working a line of tall cottonwoods erupting from the brush to the right—the favorite hideout for the timberdoodles—there was a great chance Howard would get to see his first ever. I began to say confident words to that effect when one of the tawny little birds exploded from the thick tangle to our right and flew over my head. I raised my shotgun, and the bird passed only inches from the barrel. If I had shot in this tiny little window of opportunity, the bird would have been blown to bits. It continued on its way out, peeping its way toward Greta.

"Coming at you!"

Behind me, Howard said, "What?"

He hadn't seen it, and it had nearly hit me. He must have been looking the other way. The bird ended up rocketing out behind Greta, and she never got off a shot.

With other obligations later in the morning, we sadly had to turn back. I cut into another small thicket while Greta and Howard stayed on the trail. The dogs weren't anywhere near me when a pair of birds flushed at my feet. I shot three times after the closest one and might as well have taken the shells from the chamber and thrown them at the woodcock, for all of their effectiveness. Again Howard didn't see it, and neither did Greta. They may have thought that I'd really lost it this time. I marked where the bird I'd shot at went down and decided to go after it. This entailed breaking my way farther back into this little thicket than I had ever been before. I ended up pushing in most of the way backward, shielding my face from the whipping, tugging thorns. Miraculously, when I arrived near the base of the maple tree where the bird had landed, the dogs were still with me. They flushed the bird and, in short order I missed it again. (Shell reloading is a relatively new hobby for me, and now I shook a couple of the shells before loading them into the shotgun, making sure I'd remembered to put birdshot ahead of the powder. Of course, there *was* birdshot in there, thus denying me a perfectly good excuse for my hopeless shooting.)

I joined Howard and Greta on the trail, and as we hurried down it, another bird—probably the same one I'd already flushed twice—came up from the very center of the trail. I raised my gun, as did Greta, but the bird was out of sight before we could fire.

Turning to Howard, I asked, "So, after this, are you ready to try pheasants in a week or two?"

"We'll see," he said, looking doubtful. (He never did.)

Sometimes It's Hard to Be a Good Dad

I promised the kids I'd take them out for pumpkins one Saturday morning. The thing is, I really wanted to go to the club. Now, pheasant hunting doesn't hold a candle to spending time with my kids, but I was looking for a way to compromise, so I decided I'd hit the club early and be home in plenty of time—say, 9 A.M.—for pumpkin hunting.

It was Maggie's first club hunt, and a parade of newfound friends all stopped by to check out the latest addition. Being a group of hunters inclined toward spaniels, they welcomed her more warmly than they had Ted. I enjoyed the attention lavished on her but at the same time crossed my fingers to ward off her propensity for submissive urinating. Luck and/or Maggie's bladder held out, and the floor of the clubhouse remained dry.

As on my first hunt there with Ted, gunfire erupted before we had even reached our designated hunting spot—I had traded with one of the older guys for the big open field, which is not senior-friendly. Soft calls of "Fetch it up, fetch it up!" carried through the woods. I looked at my watch and a few minutes remained before the agreed start of 7:30, so I kept Maggie heeling on the leash. We passed through a narrow lane in the hedgerow and emerged at the edge of the monstrous grass field. Maggie whined quietly when I told her to sit, but complied. I checked my watch, musing about the *civility* of this whole club thing. Then a shot went off. Dismissing civility with great pleasure, I reached down and unleashed Maggie.

Much of what happened next remains a blur. Maggie started showing interest in something near the base of an old fence post, so I put three shells into my autoloader—that much is fact. Then she ran about twenty paces straight away from me; that, too, cannot be denied. But just as I slipped the last of my questionable handloads into the chamber, I looked up to see a flushing rooster, followed closely, if briefly, into the air by my dog. The bird came down in a rain of feathers. Maggie brought the big cock and put it down near her leash, which was still at my feet, not having been stuffed yet into the game bag. I looked at my watch.

Seven-thirty.

Smiling like someone who should undergo psychiatric evaluation, I plodded on down the field. Maggie was bouncing as if she had four pogo sticks attached to her legs. Success does wonders for a dog's morale. Some fifty yards farther on, Maggie bore hard to the right and stopped bouncing. A second later, she began jerking back and forth. I walked up on her quickly, watching her sort out the scent trail in the long grass. Assuming she was just working the scent from the rooster we had already killed, I almost didn't notice when she shot in a beeline straight away from me, toward the cattle field on the neighboring property. I had always tried to stay away from the hedgerow bordering the neighbor because if a bird flushed wild across there, it wasn't legal to take it or even set foot across the fence. I knew I would have a hard time explaining that to Maggie or Ted as they raced after a rapidly departing pheasant.

Ten yards shy of the electric fence, Maggie began jerking back and forth again, her motions so violent it seemed her head would spin right off her body. I got the shotgun ready. The bird came up close, flying rapidly for the fence. I dropped it right next to the electric wire. Several huge, reddish cattle eighty yards up the fence line turned with dull interest to watch Maggie retrieve the bird. Again she dropped it impatiently at my feet, spitting out feathers and quickly turning back to hunt.

Seven-forty, and for all practical purposes I was done.

I have watched guys battle their bird dogs, and I've done it a time or two myself, but the wise course of action is to follow your dog, not lead it. It involves a lot less whistling and yelling and headache, and leaves you feeling less angry and your dog less browbeaten at the end of a hunt. So when I tried directing Maggie away from the cattle pen and back into the interior of the club property and she refused, I followed her lead

A fine rooster in fall plumage.

patiently along the north-reaching stretches of the electric fence. She wasn't birdy, but she worked doggedly up the fence, never veering back into the field or showing any sign of returning to her normal, pretty quartering. I made a few halfhearted efforts to guide her away from the fence, but she would just glance at me with what can only be described as gentle impatience. She didn't really care what I did, in other words—*she* was going to run along the fence. With two heavy birds in my game bag, I had no desire to shoot another and perhaps be branded a game hog, yet at the same time, we'd been here only a few moments and I couldn't help it if Maggie was so darned good! I decided that if a bird flew, I would let it go and then put Maggie on leash and head back toward the clubhouse.

I have often said that what distinguishes a good hunter from a mediocre one is discipline. (That's why I consider myself a mediocre hunter.) So when a hen took off, reflexes took over. Well, let me back up and say that in a fleeting moment between the flapping of wings and the raising of my shotgun, I seriously considered not shooting the bird. But when it looked like it was going to flush wild off the property and over the electric fence, thereby not giving any of the other club members a chance, I shot it.

Two shells, three birds, I thought happily to myself as I ushered the suddenly cooperative Maggie back toward the clubhouse. *I should retire from bird hunting right now,* I thought, remembering back to the dismal box-consuming day of woodcock hunting with Greta not too long ago.

A hunter I had talked to in the morning over coffee emerged from the edge of the woods, crossing into the open field with his six-month-old setter puppy. Maggie, not leashed, was heeling along nicely up the trail when she suddenly broke the heel and ran toward the other hunter.

"Maggie!"

She was not stopping.

A moment later, a rooster pheasant came up not thirty yards from me. I kept my gun draped across my arm and whistled for Maggie, already in hot pursuit, to come back. Thankfully, she raced only sixty or seventy yards before turning back to me. I could see her smile from there. Snapping the leash on her, I watched the other hunter turn to go back into the woods, not wishing to disturb us, I supposed. I wanted to get his attention, so I whistled. He ignored me.

"Hey!" (I really wished I had gotten his name.)

He turned back to me with a puzzled look that grew even more puzzled when he saw Maggie had been leashed.

Approaching us, he said, "Did you mark that one? He went down near that oak thicket."

"I know, but we've already got a few. I thought you might want to take your pup."

His face, until now a dull mask, broke into a surprised, appreciative smile.

"Well, thanks."

"Sure. Good luck."

While the dogs exchanged sniffs, we exchanged names, and I'd just turned to get out of his way when he asked, "You got a *few?*"

"Well, I was stopping at two, but Maggie flushed one toward the fence. I figured . . . you know."

"Three?"

"Yeah."

He cast an admiring glance down at Maggie and patted her on the head. "Good dog, aren't you?"

Yep, I thought, beaming.

Back at the clubhouse, I looked at my watch—only a quarter past eight. I sat up on the deck and drank coffee, talking with a very old member who had hunted for only a few minutes before his leg gave out on him. He reminisced about his dad's and his grandfather's quail dogs down south. Out of his wallet came an ancient, faded picture of two Brittanies and a pile of birds. *Those were the days.*

A trio of men worked two springers across the field nearest the clubhouse, and snippets of their conversation drifted to us on the wind. They eventually turned toward us, and I could see tail feathers sticking out of all of their vests. It had been a good morning. The back deck quickly filled with hunters and muddy, briar-infested dogs, and the stories of shots, good and bad, began flying. The last one to the deck was Bill, the guy with the setter pup we'd run into out in the field.

"Did you get him?" I asked.

"No, he flushed wild on us. Twice. Thanks for that, though. That was nice of you."

"Oh, sure," I shrugged, trying to give off an air of authentic nice-guyness. I can do that for only so long before lapsing into my real personality. Bill disappeared into the clubhouse and emerged with a mug full of coffee. Walking around to the front of the group, he leaned over and took Maggie by the leash, leading her a few feet away and in front of a picnic table containing some of the oldest guys in the group.

"Attention," Bill said.

Everyone turned to look.

"I would like to have this little bird dog declared an unfair advantage."

Everyone, including me, burst out laughing.

Home by 10 A.M., we were pumpkin hunting by 10:30 and had cored two extremely large and backbreaking pumpkins by 11. The kids' smiles were as wide as mine had been an hour earlier when the members of the club I hadn't yet met introduced themselves one by one. Later on, we picked up the crocks from our family cemetery plot and stood for a moment or two at the graying headstones, remembering. Later yet, at supper, we had fresh pheasant while the Unfair Advantage and Ted slept soundly at my feet under the table.

If there was ever a day that epitomized October, it was this.

Big Birds, Little Birds

The whole time I was messing with the shells, trying to separate the woodcock and pheasant loads that had somehow become dreadfully mixed, Maggie paced the back of the truck. Every now and then she'd charge right up to me, her split brown-and-white face and bright eyes stopping only inches from me. The whole way to the club, instead of curling up on the blankets, Maggie stayed bolt upright, front paws on the wheel well, trying to peek around the front of the truck, knowing where we were going.

When we got out at the club, two guys were trapshooting, something Maggie had never experienced before. Normally pretty good at staying with me, she strained to stifle her instinct to run and fetch the orange birds that flew across the field only eighty yards from us as shotguns roared. She looked from the field to me as if asking, "Is *that* what we're hunting for today?" Suspecting she was about to break for the shooters, I imposed a measure of safety (for both her and the orange birds) and put her on the leash. She whimpered, looking back over her shoulder at the trap field as we headed for the seclusion of the hunting fields.

Once afield and off the leash, Maggie roared off. My only gripe with her over the years is her tendency to be a bit rangy when hunting with Ted; she prefers to hunt forty or fifty yards in front of us while Ted covers the area out to thirty yards. I have always suspected that she simply didn't want him running through any scent and finding a bird before she did. But today, without the intrusion of the Lab, Maggie worked perfectly, staying about twenty yards in front of me and responding crisply to my hand signals. Avoiding the thicker brush where Ted had proved himself the previous Saturday, I kept Maggie in the open fields, where she excels. For every two feet she went forward, she bounded another two in the air. I hadn't seen her work so hard and furiously in years. Apparently she liked the club as well as I did.

We spent ten minutes circling through some sparse rows of corn, Maggie grunting and thinking and pushing her nose along the ground, soaking in whatever scent wafted up from the grass. Even as I signaled her on down the field, she kept returning to one spot. Relenting, I went and stood in the center of the circle she was making, and I wouldn't have been surprised if a bird or a rabbit had flushed at any moment. But after a while she gave up the scent, and I wondered if, on the way in, we had flushed a bird here that had been screened by a hedgerow.

Maggie continued on, more excited than ever and a bit too enthusiastic for my sore legs. I called her back and heeled her for a moment, telling her to stay close. The harshness of her panting told me she needed a break as much as I did. We walked slowly for fifty yards, the little bird dog at my heel, and arrived at one of the shallow ponds bordering the back side of the property. Maggie suddenly broke from heel and raced down the bank of the pond. I figured she just needed some water.

I was wrong.

Maggie picked up scent at the edge of the water and raced around the pond, headed east and away from me. With her nose down, she seemed to be lifting scent off the surface of the water itself. Thinking she was on a pheasant, I trudged after her. Thankfully, she didn't get too far before the bird flushed. Expecting the coarse cackle of a pheasant, I was surprised by an odd twittering cry, not unlike that of a woodcock, as the bird rose. The snipe rocketed from the reeds and across the pond, and I chased it with the barrel of the shotgun, which barked once behind the bird and then finally hit it. The bird went down in a high arc over a small cattail island, splashing down out of sight on the other side. Maggie raced back toward me, frantically looking for direction. *"Where is it?"* her bright eyes asked.

I suddenly wished I had Ted.

Maggie has done many water retrieves for me—wild pheasants love pond and creek edges—but never any blind retrieves. Ted, though no champion retriever, at least had a vague grasp of the blind retrieve. I figured Mag could probably find the bird by her scenting abilities alone, but this one was way out there, through some thick cattails. She watched me intently as I stood over her and pointed out at the cattails, marking a straight line with my arms to where I'd seen the bird go down; then I said "Fetch." She looked like a miniature tugboat as she swam out across the big pond, and I got a bit anxious as she disappeared into the weeds. I heard a splash as she hit the open water on the far side of the island, then nothing. But only a moment passed before she appeared on my side of the reeds with the small bird in her mouth. She dropped it for a moment to take a drink, then picked it up pretty as a picture and splashed into the water, heading my way.

She dropped the bird at my feet, and I could tell she was anxious to get hunting again, but I also knew she would run herself into a heart attack if given the opportunity. I made her rest as I admired the long-billed, striped, downright silly-looking bird. "Good girl, Mag," I said, petting her head and stuffing the snipe into my pocket. No need to use the game bag. Maggie took my praise to mean, "OK, go ahead and hunt," and she plunged back into the cattails. I was about to call her to move on when two snipe erupted from the reeds nearly at my feet. I was slow getting the gun up and sent one shot after the pair with little or no hope of hitting them.

Forgiving me the miss, Maggie trotted happily on around the pond. I tried to stay alert, knowing that where one or two snipe sat, several more were likely.

Thinking the stocked pheasants were probably long gone, I directed Maggie into the edge of the woods, hoping we might find some of the woodcock Ted and I had flushed on the opener. Maggie stayed with me for a few minutes, then began cutting back behind me and angling to the pond. I'd finally resorted to the whistle to get her under control when she disappeared for the third time. A little exasperated, I backtracked toward the pond, thinking she was probably still hunting for snipe. A moment later I heard her grunting and sniffing furiously in the long grass ahead of me. She was not in sight, but I could tell where she was by the rustle of weeds and grass as she plowed through.

I heard the rooster cackle long before I saw him, and for a moment I thought Maggie had caught him in the grass. A few interminable seconds passed, but nothing happened. The weeds were still moving steadily away from me. As I began to follow the progress of the encounter up ahead—now very excited at the prospect of shooting a pheasant—the grass twenty yards from me erupted, and the big ringneck rooster appeared. I was vaguely aware of Maggie directly below the bird as I hoisted the shotgun, but as I thumbed the safety button, I became *very* aware of her.

Vaulting five feet out of the long weeds, she grabbed the rooster by its breast and snatched it back to earth before I could shoot. Trotting to me with the flailing bird, Maggie growled softly as the rooster pummeled her face with desperate wingbeats. Struggling with the bird, Maggie gave it a vicious shake just as she arrived at my boots and dropped it, stone-dead.

Soon, Very Soon

Gulping back a late-night coffee I certainly didn't need, I enjoyed the warmth of Ted curled up under my desk, his nose pressed firmly—though perhaps not wisely—into my socks. Maggie was asleep on the couch on the other side of my basement office.

The dogs looked good—tired, but good. Between the woodcock hunting and the pheasant club, they were in better shape than they had ever been going into wild-pheasant hunting season. Maggie's fat rolls usually take a week or so of hard hunting to disappear, but they had already melted away in the hard running of the past three weeks. It's amazing to think that she could lose a quarter of her weight in such a short time—the equivalent of me losing twenty-five pounds in three weeks—but I wasn't complaining and neither was she. Carrying around that extra fat for the first few days of hard hunting could not be good for her. *This year*, I thought, *the wild birds had better watch out.*

Ted always looks good, lean and muscular. I don't think he has ever retained an ounce of fat. His coat was sleek and black, and his eyes squinted tightly shut as he dreamed of some wild pursuit down a game trail, whimpering softly as his legs kicked in unison. Maggie picked her head up and stared down at her hunting partner, glancing briefly at me as if to make sure I thought Ted was acting normally. Once convinced, she stood, tightened herself into an even

Pheasant running for open ground.

smaller ball, and collapsed on the couch with her nose hidden behind her nub of a tail.

"Better now?" I asked.

The nub wagged briefly.

Upstairs, I could hear Greta walking around, getting the girls a glass of water or another blanket or any of the other things that keep young girls from getting to sleep within an hour of their bedtimes. Just before bed, Jessica came down and asked if I would take her out pheasant hunting this year again.

"I think so, sweetie. I think so."

Jessica already had the drive to be a hunter, like her mom did as a young kid. Jennifer didn't show much passion for covering ground, probably because she was still so young and her legs so small that it was tough to keep up, dampening her enjoyment. I made a mental note to take them to the club, where seeing game didn't usually require hours of walking. Jen could walk there for a half-hour and have a good chance of at least seeing a bird flush. Jessica would be happy just to be there, bird or not.

When I went up to kiss them good night, I wondered, not for the first time, what they think about this father of theirs. I'm sure not many of their friends' dads are gone for what must seem like days at a time in search of birds and countless other critters. I'm not sure that any of them have a pile of feathers and fur in their yard, like the one in our "cleaning spot" next to the ditch. But Jess and Jen just seem to expect these things, and accept them as a part of everyday life. Just as sure as the school bus shows up every morning, Dad will spend the weekend cavorting across the countryside after his dogs. Just as sure as church will start at 9:30 every Sunday morning, Dad will probably have a dead deer hanging in the tree by the swing set sometime between now and November. It's just the way things are at the Spring residence during any given autumn.

At least, that's what I *hope* they think.

Either way, as I bend over to kiss each one in her bed every night, they tell me they love me. And on nights before hunts, I hear some version of ". . . and I hope you shoot a bunch of them tomorrow."

That's all the reassurance I need.

With the house above me settling into the familiar routines of late night, and both dogs finally snoring peacefully, I looked at the mess on the desk in front of me: partially read and completely unread books, a half-finished book of my own, a pile of mostly finished magazine articles, yellow Kodak boxes of photos I should have filed months ago, and so on. The work never goes away, and at this time of the year it tends to pile up dreadfully. I am usually a diligent worker (well, *somewhat* diligent anyway), but October and November make up for those months when I actually do get some work done. There was no way I could accomplish a fraction of what I needed to do tonight, so I did the prudent thing.

I ignored it, of course.

Reaching up, I flipped the calendar forward and back between November and October, then forward to December, then back to October. The pheasant opener was coming fast.

Very soon.

Visions of club hunting and woodcock chasing faded away in the light of richer memories. I could see the gaudy birds crouching, barely visible in the long grass; could hear the grunting of the dogs as they peel back earth, working for me. I envisioned those and many other things. Sipping the coffee, I ignored the cable news channel blaring away on the small TV next to my computer. Stalking the length of my office, I scanned the framed pictures of hunts past and friends past and present, of days both glorious and hilarious—and quite often both. I ran my hand over the huge mounted rooster on my bookcase, remembering the day he ran me all over Niagara County. I wished I could make him fly again right now. In my mind's ear, I heard the cackle of the rooster as he cleared brush and suddenly appeared over the top of my barrel. I heard the shot. I remembered the rustle of brush as we hustled after him, hoping for another chance. . . ."

One more week, I thought, *one more week.*

Destiny

Getting out of the truck, I was glum—I guess we all were. It's not like this place was one of our hot spots—it wasn't—but we'd go there late in the season and chase rabbits in the snow, and every now and then during bird season, after our favorite pheasant hot spots had been thoroughly combed, we would come here for a change of scenery. John's sister-in-law owned the several dozen acres and always allowed us on to chase and shoot at whatever we were in the mood to chase and shoot at. But now she was moving, and the property was as good as sold. The paperwork would be signed in a matter of weeks. John had already talked to the would-be new owner.

Sorry, no hunting.

Parking by the old barn one last time, I eyed the broken-out end windows where we'd ambushed pigeons that one of us would scare out of the barn. Quietly, John and Brian and I loaded our guns and I walked around to set Maggie and Ted free. I wanted to tell them that we probably wouldn't be coming back here ever again, but they'd never know. It was just another day for them. I guess that sometimes it's good to just be a dog. But *I* knew, and the knowing did nothing to help my mood. It was like taking a girl out on a date, knowing she was departing for missionary work in darkest Africa the next day.

Maggie with a rare limit of woodcock.

"I wonder if we'll see any pheasants," I said.

"I almost hope we don't," replied John.

"Yeah. Almost," I said, my thoughts focused sharply on opening day. Besides, the property wasn't sold yet. Surely we could get back on here for one or two pheasant hunts in the coming weeks, after the opener. But John was right; if we did find ringnecks here, losing the place was going to hurt even more. In the past two years, I had seen only one wild rooster here during pheasant season. That day, exhausted from combing the property, we'd spotted the bird strutting across golden grass at the back of the field on far side of the road. Maggie saw it, too, and was off. I yelled for her too late and was thankful no cars were coming. The tired hunters sprinted across the road with newfound energy. Of course, like most wild birds, this one knew its territory and just vanished into the maze of hedgerows and drainage ditches, pulling us deeper and deeper into unfamiliar territory. We never did see where the rooster went. If Maggie knew, she wasn't saying. But the mere presence of that bird had been a striking rarity. Although the property held ideal cover and was surrounded by big cornfields, it just never seemed to produce pheasants. The exact same cover in Ransomville or Wilson would have produced at least a bird or two a year, but the birds just weren't here.

My reverie over, I watched as Maggie and Ted bounded into the grass to the north of the barn, and we followed them into the field. Dotted here and there were a half-dozen stands of cottonwood trees, no more than an acre apiece. We had lucked into woodcock here before, so it was no surprise when one took off from one of the stands. John took a ridiculously long shot at the departing bird, and we *were* surprised when Maggie met us halfway, carrying the dead bird.

John smirked as Brian and I rolled our eyes behind his back.

"Good girl, Maggie," I said.

"Good shot, John," John said.

"Good girl, Maggie."

The next clump of cottonwoods produced two flushes, neither of which we touched. We were surprised, not at the presence of woodcock but at their *number*. We'd always killed a few, but we had never flushed three in only ten minutes. It looked like our last date with this place was going to be a good one.

The last few clumps of cottonwood produced three more flushes, and John downed another bird.

"That's more woodcock already than I've shot in the last two years combined," John said, taking the second timberdoodle from Maggie.

"You can stop now," someone said, maybe me.

The field gave way to a thick tangle of dogwood, and we hesitated a moment at the edge before plowing in. From inside the thicket, the sound of a flushing woodcock came from the same direction as the tinkling tags on Maggie's collar. Hesitating no more, we stepped in. A bird came from under Ted's nose, and I missed it. Brian, to my left, caught it when Maggie flushed it a second time. Immediately after, she flushed another one, which flew across in front of me. I missed again, and it zagged toward John. He called Ted over, and the dog flushed it back across our front. We both missed it again, but Brian got it coming in.

We had never seen anything like it. The woodcock were everywhere. The dogs weren't rangy—even Maggie was working close. The dogwood patch must have been thick with bird scent, and it seemed we couldn't go ten yards without flushing one. In that thick cover, every flush was a test of our snapshooting abilities—mostly resulting only in showers of branches and leaves. Normally, we follow a missed woodcock. Today, it wasn't necessary. If we missed one, another was sure to flush. And most of them were flushing toward the back of the patch anyway, in the direction we were steadily working. I would never have thought it possible, but we were positively drunk on woodcock—with the early hangover-headache of listening to too many shots in close quarters.

At the back of the thicket, where it emptied out into a broken, grassy field, we stopped to count our shells. Brian was nearly out. Divvying up what we had left, we pushed on into the field and, as we did, flushed two more birds out into the open. One landed in a small cottonwood clump, the other in a large drainage ditch. As Brian and John followed Maggie to the cottonwoods, I took Ted toward the ditch. On the way, we flushed another. I followed the bird and heard a wimpy "click" as my hammer fell on an empty chamber. My gun was empty. Keeping my eye on the spot where the first bird had gone into the ditch, I stuffed three shells into the Mossberg and plodded on. Ted was panting ahead of me, but still working fast, excited. I was excited, too. What were all these birds doing here? Were they all locals? Were they flight birds pushed down by the freak cold front a few weeks ago and residing now in balmy western New York until our famous winter snows arrived? But I didn't waste much time questioning our luck. Once in the ditch, Ted instantly flushed the woodcock. It twittered and dodged, and I shot and missed repeatedly. Cursing, I reloaded the gun, feeling the dwindling shell supply in the bottom of my pocket.

"Come on, Ted," I said, trying to get him to stop sniffing the small depression where the woodcock had hidden.

But he wouldn't budge, and this time, I paid attention. When the second woodcock leaped up, I took it down with one shot. Ted retrieved it most of the way to me before stopping to gag up some feathers.

"Come on, Ted, bring it on in."

Nope.

He stood there long enough to make sure I knew where the bird was, then departed, looking for more with his long black tail wagging happily.

"Did you get that one?" Brian asked.

"*Umm* . . . yeah."

I did get one, just a *different* one.

The next field was split down the middle by a hedgerow, which itself was split by a tangled lane. I went into the center to keep the dogs in the cover. John, staying to

Heading home, early season.

the north, would catch anything that flew out, and Brian watched the southern edge, a thin strip of cover to which the birds would likely fly if they tried escaping into the neighboring woodlot. The first bird came from under John's feet, and he missed it. It passed me, and I missed it. Swinging fast, Brian connected.

"Show-off."

The next one Maggie flushed almost from under my feet. I missed it with the first shot, and as it towered up, attempting to escape the lane, Brian shot it before I could get off another one. The bird landed with a puff of feathers at Ted's feet. Surprisingly, he brought it to me, but afterward went into another gagging fit. He never does that with pheasants. Timberdoodle feathers must taste terrible.

"Brian's got the touch today," John said.

"Maybe I should just give him my shells."

On the other side of the hedgerow, Brian laughed just as Maggie flushed another past him, and he hit that one, too.

"All right, now. That's *enough*," I said. "Unload your gun and step away from the hedgerow."

"Speaking of enough . . . what is the limit, anyway?"

Woodcock? Limit? I'm not sure I had ever heard those two words together in the same sentence. What a day.

"Three apiece," I said.

"All right. Hang on."

Brian unloaded two small birds from his pocket.

John said, "I've got two, too."

I emptied my vest on the ground. I had the lion's share since the dogs always brought them to me.

"Five. Oh, boy. That's it. We're done."

"We limited? All of us?"

The voices were incredulous. Feeling a bit of that incredulity myself, I realized we had been at it for just three-quarters of an hour and we were *done.*

Back at the truck, we lined the birds up on the tailgate, a small yet impressive sight.

"I'm gonna miss this place," John said.

"But did you notice, no pheasants?" I asked.

"Yeah, I did."

"So how long do you think it will take for the guy to close on this place?"

"We won't be pheasant hunting here, I would guess. Not that it matters. Still, you'd think we'd have flushed at least *one* ringneck. Even a hen."

"You would have thought."

"At least there are the timberdoodles. But we'll probably never see a flight like this. Not for another thirty years or so."

"So let's come back tomorrow."

No one disagreed. Even Ted, who was still spitting out timberdoodle feathers, wagged his tail at the suggestion.

Making a Note of It

When you write a book, it's easy to be all knowing, all seeing, especially when months have passed and the events you are writing about have nicely aged in the smokehouse of memory. All I have to do is look at my notes for a given day, lean back, and let the memories flood into my typing fingers. You wouldn't think that written notes could belie the truth, but unfortunately, they sometimes do. Let me show you what I mean. Take a look at the first few lines of my field notes for the day

I'm about to tell you about. It was just four days before the opener of pheasant season. Take a peek:

> Went to JK's property, scouting for pheasants. The place looks great! Fields haven't been hayed and there is a stunted cornfield right in the center that he hasn't bothered to plow under. It should be a bird haven. Saw deer—rabbits. No birds, but I think they're there.

Look promising to you? To me, too, but let me tell you about that day. It was warm, far too warm, but I was anxious to scout JK's property for birds. I had seen several wild birds there over the couple of years since we'd gotten permission to hunt there, but we'd never managed to kill one. The birds always seemed to be working the corn on his neighbor's property or hiding in the wide-open hedgerows, flushing wild long before we got a decent crack at them. Also, JK had been farming the place fairly heavily the past few years, and his timing was always poor, at least for us. For example, he would begin cutting corn the day *after* pheasant season ended, not the day before. Or he would hay out the fields a week or so prior to pheasant season, forcing the big birds to seek out other cover, usually off his property. Now, mind you, I didn't blame the man at all. He was a farmer, so naturally he *farmed*, and though he didn't mind us hunting there, he was not there to provide bird habitat or birdhunter happiness. He had his priorities, and we had ours.

But this year, it looked as if we'd hit it right. I made a quick drive-by on my way to work and saw that the hayfields were still standing. The neighbor's tall corn was pushing right up against JK's hedgerows.

The little patch of last year's stunted corn had gone wild in the middle of one of the grass fields. Patches like that were always ringneck magnets. Twice during the summer I'd driven past the farm and seen wild birds poking around the periphery of the fields; one even crossed the road in front of my truck. Back then, in August, I prayed the fields would look like that come October. Finally, my prayers were answered. It appeared we had our own private two hundred acres worth of pheasant heaven. As much as I detest the things, I took a handful of posted signs and touched up the perimeter of the property.

Mine, all mine.

As the wait for the coming season dwindled slowly from months to weeks and finally to days, it was time for my wife, me, and the dogs to set foot on the solid ground of my surefire hot spot and check it out. Greta and I debated taking the guns from the truck. There were no woodcock here, and shooting rabbits in the long grass would be a near impossibility. We decided it would be hot enough walking without toting the heavy 12-gauges.

As a side note, I tell many inexperienced hunters *never* to pass up an opportunity to carry a gun, even if chances of seeing game are remote. I've drilled this into many heads, but apparently not hard enough into my own—probably due to my relative cranial thickness. It falls under the umbrellas of both Murphy's Law and Common Sense. Being unarmed during an open season is akin to loading a deer gun with only three shells when it holds six—you can be sure your first three shots will be off and you'll go home deerless.

When Greta asked, "Are you *sure* you don't want to take the guns in case we see any rabbits?" I shook my head.

"Grass is too deep. Never get off a shot."

Well . . .

Ted and Maggie slowed quickly under the shimmering heat. The grass was long and not particularly thick, but the drainage ditches running through the property were heavily choked with weeds that had escaped the past few years' mowing. Last year, right near one of JK's cattle pens, the dogs had jumped a large coyote when we were rabbit hunting. Later, JK's neighbor told me he had watched the coyote tear out of the ditch, run up his driveway, then sprint through his cows before disappearing into the cornfield beyond. "Too bad you couldn't have shot him." I'd barely even *seen* him.

Angling toward the small patch of corn gone wild, we rounded a bend and found ourselves face to face with a dozen beehives. Greta is allergic to the little buzzers and slowly backed away, all the while yelling for Ted, who was only inches from one of the hives. The air was alive with the sound of their buzzing. Ted, trailing a dozen angry bees behind him, finally came back. We skirted wide around the bees, but Greta was quiet for a few moments and I knew the close encounter had bothered her. Just last year, her arm had swelled to twice its normal size after just one sting. The sight of those thousands of bees must have really spooked her.

In the corn, it wasn't long before we were treated to the sight of the hot, tired dogs getting birdy. The sound of wings beating in the dry stalks brought an instinctive reaction—I raised my imaginary shotgun to the rising flush of three mourning doves. A moment later a couple dozen more came up. Then more. The little patch was full of them—but no pheasants. They were probably roosting in the deep cover of the long grass.

We came out the other end and found a buck rub on a large tree at the end of a hedgerow. A creature of hunting habit, I looked up, searching for a suitable place to put a tree stand. A moment later, with the dogs breaking brush in a double hedgerow, a large cottontail raced in our direction, stopping perhaps twenty feet from me and ten feet from Greta. The rabbit, deciding that we were probably not friendly, departed for the cover of the corn with Ted following closely behind. Greta shot me one of those looks. You know, the *wife* look.

"Don't say it."

"No, honey, the grass is too long," she said, trying to sound like me. But she had it all wrong, making me sound terribly whiny. Snickering, she turned and walked back toward the truck.

Out in the last open field before the road, Maggie began quartering and sniffing faster and faster. We knew she must be on something to be expending this much energy in the heat.

"Please let it be a pheasant," I said.

Nope. Rabbit. The overheated bird dog stared back at us with her tail wagging.

"Why didn't you shoot?" her brown eyes asked.

I didn't look at Greta.

Later on, after dinner, we put the kids in the truck and drove back to JK's place, just because it was hunting season and we do an awful lot of driving around and looking during hunting season. I don't know exactly why we went back there. As we turned off the main road, movement in the back of one of JK's fields caught my eye. Just at the edge of the woods in the waning light of day, a large eight-point buck was moving about in plain sight. I passed the binoculars back to the girls, who eyed the deer approvingly.

"Can you deer hunt here?" Greta asked.

"Yep," I said, smiling.

The buck quickly got nervous and began moving back into the shade of the woods. Putting the truck in gear, I moved on up the road, against the protests of Jessica and Jennifer.

"Gotta let him eat, girls. I don't want to scare him off his food."

"That way he'll be good and fat when we eat *him*," Jennifer chimed in.

"Noooo, we just want to let the buck eat in peace."

The girls giggled.

We turned a corner along JK's property, and my heart sank. He was haying the field we had walked through only a few hours earlier.

"Damn," I hissed under my breath, mindful of the girls.

"Well, it's not like we saw any birds anyway," Greta said.

"Yeah, but now we probably never will—at least not this year."

Journal entry (continued):

Went back in the evening with the girls. Saw a nice buck near CT road. Also saw JK haying the place. We just can't win. No birds again this year.

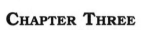

CHAPTER THREE

THE MAIN EVENT

Monday—Wild Pheasant Season—Finally

It was cold. It was wet. The gray skies promised to make it colder and wetter before the day was through, but at least and at last we were here. As we loaded up, I noticed a dozen or so cats wandering around outside Betty's barn and wondered how many more must be inside. Last year I'd found no fewer than ten cat skeletons out here in the open field, the coyotes apparently having taken it upon themselves to act as feline population-control in the area.

Brian and I set out under the gloomy skies into the long grass near Betty's house and were instantly soaked. It hadn't rained for several hours, but the wet grass drenched us in mere seconds, and the cold north wind completed the refrigeration effect. Brian was smiling in his new waterproof brush pants, and I was frowning in my old water-*absorbent* ones. It didn't matter. In moments the water began gushing from the sky and permeated every inch of our clothing, waterproof or not.

The dogs didn't seem to mind, zipping madly through a field they hadn't set foot in since our summer voyage out here. If anything, the conditions made them even zippier. If it was me running through the field with only my body hair for a shield, I'd be moving mighty fast myself, if somewhat more carefully.

Discussing a plan of attack was an idea better left for inexperienced bird hunters. Our plan was to simply follow the dogs. It is the most productive way to get birds. The only wrinkle was that around 9:30 we would have to angle back toward the road to pick up Greta, who'd be joining us once the kids were on the bus. In my own defense, yes, we *could* have waited for Greta and begun hunting at 9:30 ourselves. Giving up a couple of miserably wet hours afield so that we all could begin at the same time might seem to be the genteel mode of behavior. But, get real, man, this was opening day, and Greta never even suggested it. She's very understanding of such things.

We covered the first dozen acres in roughly a straight line. The dogs, eating up ground and quartering us perfectly, picked up nothing. Two hours gone. We shook our heads. I thought about going back to the truck to call Greta and tell her to forget it, that we'd come back and drink coffee and hope the sun came out. My watch, though, said it was already 9:15, so she would be on her way. Oh, well. Might as well start steering the dogs back to the road to meet her. We passed through a small thicket on the north side of the woods and prepared for the inevitable woodcock flushes. Last year we'd flushed a half-dozen out of here. And after the dozens we'd seen at John's sister's place, I had high hopes.

But again, nothing—not even a timberdoodle.

Halfway back to the road, Ted started turning and quartering, sniffing and shifting positions. *Finally.* I didn't care if it was just a smelly old rabbit. We needed something to show for our boots full of rain. When the critter shot out of the dogwood clump to my right, as yet unseen by the dogs, I sighed and called out to

Brian, "It's just a cat." His body posture changed, and his gun barrel drooped back toward the earth.

"*This* way, Maggie, Ted," I said, hand-signaling the dogs away from the cat scent before we were treated to a cross-country race that would undoubtedly end in a hissing, treed cat and two happy yet exhausted dogs. Surprisingly, the dogs listened to me, and we headed due south, back to the road. Sixty or seventy yards from where we'd jumped the cat, Maggie was suddenly growling, and a flash of gray caught my eye.

"The cat?" Brian asked.

"I guess. . . ."

Before I could positively identify the creature Maggie was shadowing by mere inches, the grass erupted in what can only be accurately described as a real-life depiction of the cartoon Tasmanian Devil. A ball of dog and some other species rolled past me in the grass, growling and hissing and barking and snapping. Teeth were gnashing. If this was a cat Maggie was tangled up with, it was the King of All Cats.

Stupidly stepping into the mix, I yanked Mag's collar when it came into view and pulled her away from the fray. The sharp teeth of an extremely large raccoon missed my right hand and Maggie's neck by inches. Spinning back around, I landed a kick into the chest of the oncoming coon, at the same time yelling at the recharging Maggie. Threading my foot under Maggie's chest, I flipped her over backward and spun to face the coon again. Puffed up like an adder, its hair standing on end, it lunged toward me. I'd never shot an animal in self-defense before, and hope I don't ever have to again. Even with two loads of No. 6 birdshot delivered at four yards, the coon was mostly undeterred. At the third shot, it lay still, one foot from my left boot.

I looked up at Brian, who was staring at me, his mouth agape. He was only yards away but had no idea what was going on down in the grass in front of me.

"Raccoon. *Very* angry."

"Oh," he said quietly, nodding.

Grabbing Maggie's collar, I led her away from the carcass and into a small opening in the long grass. Ted followed closely, wanting nothing to do with the dead coon. I made Maggie lie down, and we went over her, looking for tooth marks or cuts or blood. Miraculously, there were none.

A moment later, Greta's little blue car pulled up on the roadside a hundred yards away. I was ready to leave and try somewhere else, but with Greta loading her shotgun and heading our way, I guessed it wouldn't hurt to make a few more loops through the field. I made a mental note of the dead raccoon's location so we could avoid it.

"How are you doing?" Greta asked.

"No birds, but one big dead raccoon."

"Maggie?"

"Yeah, they were rolling down the field together like a giant basketball."

"Oh, no . . . did you check her for . . .?"

"Yes, dear."

"Find birds," she said, taking Maggie's little brown-and-white face in her hands. "*Birds.*"

Brian and I laughed. I've always said that Maggie would hunt anything if you let her. I've killed ducks and geese and squirrels and birds and rabbits with her, but this was a first. I was just glad we didn't live in grizzly territory.

The three of us circled the field twice, and the rain let up once again, giving way to a harsh wind from the north. We were all chilled. At one of the back hedgerows, I spotted a squirrel running through the lower branches of a row of red oaks. It stopped to cut a nut, and I tried pointing it out to Greta, who was close behind me. Brian was still out in the field.

"See that tree? No, that one . . . on that lower branch . . . no, not *there*."

Greta has the best hunter's eyes of anyone I've ever known—and good-looking ones to boot—but she just could not see that squirrel. A second later its tail twitched as it turned to face us, knowing something was wrong. I lifted my gun and dropped the squirrel from the tree.

"See, Greta?" Brian said. "See how he is? He does that to me all the time."

Rolling my eyes, I sighed as Maggie suddenly materialized under the tree, scooping the squirrel up and delivering it nicely to my feet. The mighty bird hunters were reduced to bushy-tail shooting.

Walking the edge of a cornfield for pheasants.

"OK, let's head over to the firehall fields," I suggested. "We're not seeing anything here."

Back near the road, the dogs became birdy once again, not far from Betty's barn.

"No cats!" I yelled. "Birds, Maggie. Birds, Ted!"

The dogs were working themselves into a frenzy as we grew closer and closer to the road. Jogging to keep up with them, all three of us had hopes that a big old rooster pheasant was about to salvage the morning.

"Rabbit!" I yelled as Ted pounced near my feet and a large cottontail catapulted from a clump of grass. It cleared an opening fifteen yards from me and I shot, kicking up dirt several feet behind it. Maggie spotted the hopping bunny, but Brian stopped it with a single shot before she could close the distance. Maggie fetched the rabbit to him, and Ted walked along, sniffing its fur and sneezing.

"A squirrel and a rabbit—that's *something*, anyway," I said.

We deposited the two furbearers in a cooler in the back of the truck and let the dogs eat a few handfuls of jerky.

"Shame about the coon," Greta said. "Was he a big one?"

"Yeah, he was *huge*."

"Was the fur worth saving?"

I explained the three point-blank shots.

"Oh."

After downing a quick cup of convenience-store coffee, we walked out to the fields behind the firehall. It was one of the places Maggie and I had cut our teeth chasing birds. But that was then and this was now. The long-grass fields of that first year had given way one by one to cabbage and corn and other crops. The stout hedgerows lining the fields still held some pheasants, and the few fields that were allowed to go fallow occasionally produced a bright wild bird. The place's downfall, particularly on a wet day, was access—it took a long walk down a clay tractor path to get there. Before we were even halfway to the first hedgerow, each of our boots wore ten pounds of mud. It felt like we were walking on Jupiter (you know, lots of gravity). The dogs slipped and slid and turned dark gray from the mud, occasionally darting into the cut cabbage field for traction or a quick sniff.

The hedgerow, thick and nasty, was still there, with a stunted cornfield on one side. It looked promising. Our hips and legs ached from fighting the sucking mud, but we pushed on into the lumpy, rutted fields along the row. I ordered the dogs into the brush, and they disappeared, their locations revealed by tag-tinkle and snapping twigs. Every now and then the leathery beating of wings would cause the guns to come up, but it would be a dove or a cardinal. The hedgerow seemed overpopulated with bright male cardinals, splendid in their scarlet fall colors—which, I might add, when glimpsed out of the corner of your eye don't look unlike a rooster pheasant.

"Rabbit!" Brian yelled from the other side of the hedgerow. I jumped. Then, "No. Jeez . . . it's another coon!"

Through the thick row, I could just make out the low, shambling shape of a small raccoon headed south up the hedgerow as the dogs headed north. I couldn't believe they hadn't seen it. Either that or they had a strong aversion to tangling with another one. That would be OK, too.

Shortly after—wet, cold, and miserable—we went for lunch at the local Polish Family Restaurant. None of us is Polish, and the place has no real charm for us, but somehow over the past five years it has become the lunch stop on opening day of pheasant season. The food there may be good—I don't really know since I only go there once a year—but it was a warm place to come in out of the cold. Unfortunately, what the small tavern/restaurant lacked in atmosphere (none), it didn't make up for in menu diversity. The waitress— I'm quite certain she was the same woman who served us every year—was pleasant enough, but our ordering had no diversity either:

"Hi, guys, what would you like? Drink to start?"

"Could I get a Diet Pepsi, please?"

"*Ummmm*, no."

"Root beer?"

A shake of her blonde head and an apologetic shrug.

It seemed that only one brand of soda was anywhere within a hundred miles, and she was going to make me ask for every last one before I finally hit the jackpot.

"What do you have?"

"Hang on."

Unbelievably, she left, coming back a moment later to recite three brand names, one of which I recognized. The rest of the ordering went no better. By the time my drink order had been finalized, Brian and Greta had pretty much decided what they wanted to eat. The waitress smiled and mentally took their orders. Then it was my turn. This led, unfortunately, to another exchange rivaling my drink order.

"I'd like the Reuben sandwich."

"Sorry, no corned beef today."

I frowned, and then realized that this was the same conversation we'd had last year. Continuity is important, I guess.

"OK, then the fish sandwich."

When our waitress grabbed her nose and shook her head emphatically, I was sure I was on *Candid Camera*.

"Bad?"

"Probably . . . it's been a while since anyone ordered fish."

Of course.

"So what would *you* recommend?"

At this she brightened and sold me the Chicken Finger Platter with the enthusiasm of someone who was making at least 50 percent commission for every last damn chicken finger she sold.

"Fine, thanks."

Later on, when the meal was just a greasy memory, Greta and Brian, Maggie and Ted, and I were all ankle-deep in the muck of another of our pheasant-hunting paradises. Following the old railroad bed to the fields hadn't been bad, since the dirt there was hard-packed from years of tractors and ATVs and hunters, but once we stepped off it, it was the same old ankle-sucking muck all over again. This place was interesting, though, and always seemed worth the long walk to get there. We'd created many fine bird-hunting memories here, and it seemed entirely possible, even under these gloomy circumstances, that we might actually flush a wild rooster here. The place had a history for us.

It was several hundred acres of cornfields and hayfields sprinkled with a handful of ponds and crisscrossed by four large hedgerows wide enough to offer ample cover to the pheasants that thrived here. I couldn't tell you how many birds and ducks and rabbits we've shot there over the years, but it was enough to bring us back in the cold rain today.

One interesting thing about this farm plot was the presence of bobwhite quail. Over the past few years, we've flushed several coveys there. If you are from the South, this revelation might not astound you, but since quail aren't a legal gamebird anywhere in New York State (with the exception of Long Island, several hundred miles from here), it is a fact worth noting.

We worked steadily along the corn, listening to Maggie and Ted racing up and down the rows, hidden by the seven-foot-high stalks. At any moment a bird might come out, and despite our poor luck so far, we were alert enough to keep our guns at the ready. Luck can turn on a dime. One minute we could be cursing the muses, and the next we might be desperately trying to rip off a shot at a rapidly departing rooster. But as we reached the end of the third cornfield and watched the dogs emerge from the stalks muddy and sullen, we began to doubt our chances.

"OK," I said. "Let's go to the ditch leading out of the pond."

I'd wanted to leave that spot for last. Every year we kill two or three roosters in the tight confines of that narrow drainage. But by the looks on my partners' faces, it was time for all or nothing.

The pond's excess water runs through the center of the cornfields by way of a small ditch. The ditch is choked with wild grass and brambles and is completely hidden from view by the tall corn. I've never seen a bootprint other than mine in the mud along its edge. The birds, full of corn and feeling safe and secure, hunker down in the shade of the prickers and wild wheat and wait out the day until it's time to go back into the corn and feed again. This wet, nasty day seemed a perfect time to find them in the thick cover, waiting for the sun to shine again. I'd wanted to wait until the end of the day, knowing or at least fervently hoping we could kill a bird there.

It was time to play that card now.

I heeled the dogs through the corn, since they probably knew where we were headed and would undoubtedly be happy to go there without me. Once we three gunners had broken out into the relatively open ditch, I let the dogs go. They dove into the ditch, and I found my heart racing. This was just one of those places. It never failed. Well, it rarely failed. Hardly ever failed?

Today, it failed.

The dogs worked the length of the ditch from its origin at the pond to where it spread out in muddy fingers through the cornfield. They scented nothing.

"If we can't find a bird *here*," I said, "I'm about ready to call it a day."

To my disappointment, no one disagreed.

Slanting back toward the road, we cut the corner of a logged-off woodlot, where the dogs poked around without any real enthusiasm. I was hoping for at least a woodcock or a rabbit to shoot at or even to see, but nothing. As we mucked our way through a low spot in the field, I became aware of a strange sound in the corn to our right. The dogs had gone in not far from there, but the sound was more substantial than even the massive, blockheaded Ted parting the cornstalks. It sounded like a bulldozer coming our way. Brian, Greta, and I stopped and listened as the sound grew closer.

"What the hell?" someone asked.

"The dogs?" I asked.

"No . . . listen. . . ."

The corn ten yards from me parted, and the largest white-tailed buck I've ever seen exploded from the stalks and ran between Brian and me. At least ten antler points adorned its head, and each of the tines reached seven or eight inches above the main beam. But getting an accurate judgment of his antlers was difficult due to the fact that he was carrying a dozen long cornstalks in his antlers. He paused briefly, thirty yards from us in the opening, before gracefully bounding twice to disappear back into the corn on the opposite side of the mud hole. Dumbfounded, we walked over to his tracks, which were wide and splayed and pressed deeply into the rich, black earth along the edge of the field.

"Wow!" we all agreed.

I've hunted deer a long time, some of it in woods not very far from here, but have never seen such a buck. He was true record-book material.

Following the narrow lane between the corn and the woodlot, we ran into another hunter and a younger guy who appeared to be his son.

"Did you see him?" I asked.

"The deer? Yeah," said the older hunter, clad in a red plaid Woolrich coat.

He looked guilty, as if we might be about to kick his butt off this piece of privately owned land. They didn't appear to have dogs, yet they were armed with decent shotguns.

"What are you hunting, rabbits?" I asked.

"Pheasants," he answered glumly.

"No dog?"

"No, but it doesn't seem to matter. I don't think there's any birds around. We've been out all day and haven't seen a damned thing."

I resisted the urge to ask how he expected to see any pheasants in a cornfield without the aid of a dog or two. Perhaps he was one of those hunters who could clearly recall those "old days" when the sky was dark with pheasants and you needed only to open your game bag and wait for one or two roosters to crash-land in your pouch. The boy's face held a bored look.

"Good luck," I said.

And I meant it. If anyone needed some luck, it was those two. On the way out, we discussed trying another property before dark, but all concurred that it might be better to go home and dry off and start fresh tomorrow. Conditioned or not, even the dogs looked worn. We reflected on the day. If we'd been strictly *mammal* hunting, you could rationalize that it had been something of a success. We'd managed to bag a squirrel, a rabbit, and a raccoon and were nearly trampled by the biggest white-tailed buck any of us had ever laid eyes upon. The day had not been an utter flop.

But still, one more opening day was over with no birds to show for it, and it would be a long time until the next opener.

Tuesday

In my admittedly subjective memory at least, many bird-hunting days have been of the *Outdoor Life* magazine cover variety: blue skies, orange trees in the background, knee-high golden grass, and a flushing bird, if not a few. But this year our representative cover photo would need to be taken with a special camera—the underwater kind. It seemed we were just destined to be wet. Much like opening day, Tuesday was troubled not so much by the tiny amount of rain in the air as by the inescapable wetness of *everything.* I could imagine the birds hunkered down in the most waterproof cover they could find, and that wasn't likely to be out here in the middle of a grass field. But still, we had killed birds here in other years under similar conditions, so Brian and John and I plodded along behind the dogs with a faint, if soggy, sense of hope.

Halfway to the far reaches of the field, where it began to dissolve into saplings and hardwood thickets, we found ourselves ankle-deep in water for several dozen yards. The grimaces on my partners' faces were undeniable. Even Maggie tiptoed through the icy water, which was certainly doing unpleasant things to her pink, exposed belly skin. Only Ted seemed to be truly enjoying himself, tearing up and down the miniature lake like a speedboat in a bathtub. Though goofy and happy, I don't think he attained his full degree of pleasure until he had done a fly-by of each of his human counterparts, spraying them from head to toe with water and throwing his head up to enhance the effect.

"Ted!" I said, exasperated. After the five years of his life, I would have expected some of the puppiness to have leached from his system. So far, though, no go.

Just as I was about to lash him with harsher words, he began working scent, or at least appearing to. I was suspicious: He and Maggie had both mastered the ploy of "Oh, wait, there's some game," right about the time they knew they were going to get yelled at. I doubted Ted's honesty, but held back on further rebukes. When the Lab did several hard double takes, still sloshing around in four or five inches of water peppered with clumps of wild wheat, I took him seriously. Even Maggie read his body language and splashed over to see what was the matter.

While John sloshed toward higher terrain, Brian and I stood our soggy ground and watched the dogs work. After two days of wet misery, we were not about to let a rooster flush unattended. When the bird finally blasted off from the square end of Ted's nose, both of our guns came up. I shot and missed what at first glance appeared to be a woodcock. It twittered straight up into the heavens before circling once around us in a hundred-yard arc and disappearing over the far woods.

"Woodcock?" Brian asked.

"Close," I said, picking up my shell. "It was a snipe."

Brian shrugged and turned back to follow John and the dogs to higher ground. I'd often seen snipe in puddles like this on such days, but the rain and general lack of high spirits in our group stopped me from explaining.

We worked the field all the way to the back and then halfway back to the road, nearly to the spot where I'd killed the coon yesterday. Not a flush. Better than an hour had elapsed, and I was ready for even the odd snipe-flush to break the wild-bird hunting stalemate we had endured so far. Along the field's edge was a thick row of dogwoods, from which a couple of roosters had earned a ride home in the game bag last year. We pushed it up and pushed it down. No birds. I thought surely that the pheasants would be taking cover in there. Beyond that, rising like a yellow sea was a field I'd just recently secured permission to hunt. In previous years, many of the birds we'd flushed on this place and either not shot at or missed had landed in there. I'm not prone to trespassing, so I finally found the landowner and got his blessing to hunt the place.

The new field looked as good as anything else we'd tried. I didn't believe that the birds would be sitting out in the open, but I had seen stranger things and was willing to give the unlikely prospect a shot. Brian and John were as agreeable as they ever get as we set foot onto the brand-new land. What appeared from a distance to be another forgotten overgrown field turned out to be heavily gouged by years-old tractor ruts. We crossed against the grain of the ruts, and each step had us either jumping from elevated point to elevated point or twisting and slipping down into the boot-sucking mud in the bottom of the ruts. It was unpleasant and treacherous walking, and my hips began to ache, but I could easily imagine all manner of pheasant and rabbit and other critters running up and down these ruts, using them as escape corridors

Which way did they go?

and hiding cover. No wonder it was one of the first places the birds headed when we missed them. They could land in here, hit the ground running, and go for three-quarters of a mile down one of the ruts without ever poking their heads above dog's-eye level.

The field eventually—and thankfully—dumped out through another hedgerow and into a familiar cornfield that had produced many birds for us in past years. It was one of the last big cornfields that I knew of in Niagara County where many hedgerows still crisscrossed through the stalks, providing ample cover and travel lanes for deer and turkeys and pheasants. We considered doing one of our usual pushes down through the corn, but the bit of walking we did through the stalks left us soaked from head to toe. We quickly agreed to once again brave the equally unpleasant rutted field and head back toward the other property.

Maggie hadn't joined us for quite some time when we emerged from the corn, and I suspected she was running down a pheasant in the impossible tangle of stalks and ears. When she finally did catch up with us, she was panting heavily, and every inch of her white fur was coated with mud.

Crossing the ruts the second time seemed somehow more unpleasant than on the first pass—probably because we'd done all that ankle twisting and hip busting without a single empty shell, much less a bird, to show for it. Once free of the ruts, we took a break in the lane along the dogwood hedgerow. We were cold, tired, sore, and generally miserable, but in the end I knew I'd picked my hunting partners well: Neither of them wanted to quit.

Yet.

Liking the prospects of hunting something thorn-free and relatively rutless for an hour or so, we picked a couple of fairly open, flat areas. Nice for pictures, sure, with their sparse golden grass and level walking, but they were useless for pheasants, and I was relieved when they gave way to the back of Betty's field and the beginnings of the slash that eventually led to a large patch of hardwoods. Shouldering through a couple of acres of beech saplings, we threaded our way along, walking three abreast and fifty yards apart. Our destination was a thorn patch on the far side of the property, but we never made it. The first woodcock went up in a flurry of wing beats. I emptied two shells after it, and either Brian or John, perhaps both, peppered it when it flew past them. Maggie retrieved it handily—to me, of course—much to the chagrin of the two who might actually have hit the thing.

"Nice bird."

We allowed that the woodcock might be a fluke, even given our stellar day of 'doodle shooting at John's sister-in-law's soon-to-be-lost property. Acclimated to generally bad woodcock hunting, we really didn't think that this, the second day of pheasant season and quite late into the woodcock flight, would give us good shooting. As has often been the case in my hunting career, however, I was delighted to find myself wrong. By the time the third bird went up and then was scooped up in Ted's great black maw, where it looked about the size of a house wren, we were begging No. 7½ shotshells from Brian. John and I had each killed a bird, but the pheasant loads were a bit too heavy. None of the birds we'd taken was so damaged as to be inedible, but I attribute that to the fact that none of the hits had been direct. Thank goodness for poor wingshooting.

The other thing I was thankful for that day was the apparent end of Brian's hot streak on woodcock. He missed as many as John and I, and I would like to believe he missed even *more.*

Woodcock are tough to get with flushing dogs. Ted works close and makes the shooting somewhat bearable, but Maggie is more rangy and tends to put up birds at thirty or forty yards—ideal for pheasants in open cover but too far to try and hit a four-inch target zigzagging in heavy saplings where you are often lucky merely to get your gun up, much less get a shot off.

But even with pheasant dogs, pheasant guns, and pockets full of pheasant loads, we managed to kill some woodcock. Unbelievably, we killed our limit again. Before lunch, the three of us had nine birds.

"Pheasants tomorrow?" I asked.

"Or woodcock," Brian mused.

"You know what will happen if we go out with guns full of eight-shot," I said. "We'll be seeing pheasants all day."

"Bring some sixes then."

The conversation dragged on into the afternoon as we celebrated our second smashing day of woodcock hunting. When we finally retreated for home some hours later, tomorrow was still up in the air.

Pheasants or woodcock?

Wednesday, Pheasants, with a Capital P

It was, after all, the third day of pheasant season, and to leave the house with the sole intent of pursuing the suddenly abundant woodcock would be to accept the possibility that we weren't going to get any pheasants. That simply could not be the case. We'd had hard opening weeks before, although I don't ever recall *two* straight days without the killing of a wild bird. But, hell, that's why they call it hunting, not shooting—as most hunters working on a stellar losing streak are wont to say. Besides, if I'd just wanted to have the relative certainty of at least seeing a pheasant, I could always swing by the club. But the time for that was past. This was opening week of wild-bird season. And it was as it always had been: short, sweet, and hard on man and dog alike. No, today we were going for pheasants, despite the odds and despite the woodcock. We were *pheasant hunters,* first and foremost. We were *not* hunting woodcock. Absolutely not. (Before Brian pulled in the driveway, I shamefully tossed a handful of woodcock loads into a hidden pocket inside my vest, suspecting we might need them.)

Pulling his hunting pants on by the trunk of the car, Brian asked, "Where to?"

"Let's try here."

He looked skeptical, but no more so than I felt. I figured that if our cross-field journeys in the other corners of the county hadn't paid off, maybe it was time to try close to home.

At the time we bought our little house in Newfane, it had been a months-long struggle to find a place that we could afford. So when we happened across the nondescript ranch house near the end of a road and not far from a gunshop, I felt good about it. Suffice it to say that I nearly fell out of my chair when the realtor told me the price over the phone. We could afford it! Our first venture into the house was on a bitter winter day. My dad, John, and a very pregnant Greta were in the party. We all seemed to approve of the place. We did stuff like look at the heater and knock on pipes and look under sinks. It didn't really mean all that much to me because, as you now know, *we could afford it!*

Pulling out of the driveway after our apparently thorough investigation of the house, we drove up the road to see what the neighbors' places looked like. Most were nondescript little ranch houses, presumably owned by people who could afford them. It turned out to be a mellow little side road and generally looked like a pleasant place to live, but the one thing that impressed me was the enormous, gaudy rooster pheasant fluffed up against the cold and sitting in a bush in a scrappy tangle of vines between two of my future neighbors' houses. I should note that at the time I'd never really hunted birds, deer being my only avidly pursued prey, but the sight of that rooster in a thicket that would one day become a favorite rabbit hunting spot of mine somehow spoke to me. We made an offer on the house within a week.

As we rounded the bend past my shed and headed out into a neighbor's big field, I felt several pangs of doubt. I loved hunting out here, had killed deer and countless rabbits and even a few woodcock, but sadly, I could remember every pheasant I'd flushed here in the eight years since we'd moved in. There were the two hens I flushed shortly after buying the property. There were three or four hens that had gone up in the big field when we were woodcock hunting. One year a monstrous rooster had come up from behind a log when I assumed that Ted was rooting out a rabbit for me. And last year I hadn't seen a one, although occasionally the cackle of a cockbird was carried to me on the breeze at sunset while I was bowhunting deer. They were out there, all right, but not in any numbers. While I was gone to Maine bear hunting in

September, Greta had taken Ted out for a walk here and he'd promptly flushed a beautiful rooster for her, one she says she could have killed with a stone. But when I took the dogs out for a little reconnaissance in the weeks leading up to wild-bird season, we didn't flush a single pheasant. So why were Brian and I beginning this long, tiring walk out to the home fields? I honestly did not know, but I didn't tell Brian that.

Maggie and Ted coursed the field nicely, but I noticed from a distance that Ted's left eye seemed to be sagging a bit. He had exceptionally red, droopy eyes for a Lab, so I didn't pay it much attention. When he swung by me for a pat on the head, I gave his eye a quick look, plucked out several of the tiny seed pods that collect in the corners of both dogs' eyes every time we're out, and sent him on his way, seemingly none the worse for wear and certainly no less happy to be hunting.

As we approached the thick hedgerow bordering the field on the south, I noticed Maggie putting on speed. Nothing fancy, not yet birdy, she was just working a bit farther out than I liked. It isn't uncommon for her to get like this in sparse cover, as if she's impatient with places she knows aren't likely to hold birds and isn't inclined to trust my judgment. Everyone compliments great field hunters on being "thinking dogs," and while I do think Maggie is one of the great ones, I often wish she'd leave just a *little* more of the thinking to me. Enjoying the warmth of a dry, blue-sky October day—one we richly deserved after Monday and Tuesday—I was loath to blow apart the tranquil scene by letting rip with my whistle. Unfortunately, as Maggie became a smaller and smaller speck out ahead of us, I had to fumble under my T-shirt and seize the cord of the little black whistle. She was nearing full flight now, and the whistle didn't even slow her down. Diving headlong into the hedgerow, she headed up it before we were even within sixty yards.

"Is she birdy?" Brian asked.

"I dunno, maybe a rabbit." The thick hedgerow was positively polluted with cottontails.

Taking no cue from me—we've hunted together long enough to know each other's moves—Brian busted brush through the hedge and paralleled me on the other side. I jogged along, trying to catch up with my errant bird dog, then momentarily stopped and listened for her. Nothing, save for the occasional snap of a twig far out ahead. Had to be a rabbit, just had to be. Even Ted was sprinting up the row, paying me no attention, a sure sign that they were on some very fresh scent. Ted didn't often abandon me unless game was around.

I heard the beating wings a split-second before the rooster's cackle and the dry *whap-whap* of Brian's autoloader, strangely muted by the wind direction and the dense hedge.

"So?"

"Too far out. Maggie's *way* out there."

"Damn. We should have come at it into the wind. We let that bird run Maggie all the way down the row."

"Yeah," Brian agreed. "What the hell is wrong with you?"

When Maggie finally returned with Ted in tow, only Ted looked guilty. I bent over Maggie and went through the mental anguish of wanting to yell at her and at the same time praise her for squeaking a bird out of this hopeless place. If I had a dollar for every time I've looked at her with that same mixture of conflicting emotions, I wouldn't be carrying a cheap shotgun. We quickly worked the cover where the bird appeared to have flown, but to no avail. He was long gone. On the way back to the main fields, Ted kicked up a woodcock that gave Brian a futile shot as it flashed through some thick dogwoods.

Back at the house, we pondered what to do next— like hit one of the woodcock spots or one of the state parks where they usually stock a handful of birds. I turned Ted's head back and forth in the thin ray of sunlight penetrating the door next to the kitchen table. His left eye was decidedly cloudy. Supposing he'd taken a stick in the eye, I checked around the edges of his pupil and fished out a couple of innocent-looking seeds with my fingertip. Turning his eye back into the light made him wince.

"I think Ted's out of commission for a couple of days."

As we drove the ten miles to one of our wild-bird fields at the four-corners of two back roads near where I grew up, I was constantly distracted by Maggie's frenetic pacing in the back of the truck. I just assumed she was happy to be rid of Ted so she could show off for Brian and me. She

Rooster pheasant making a woodland getaway.

certainly was excited. Her whimpers carried through the double-glass windows of the truck and cap. I was excited, too, after finally seeing a wild bird that morning. Unfortunately, the sight of two orange vests and one bounding dog methodically working the center of our chosen field took the wind out of my sails.

"Where now?" Brian asked.

I didn't know. "What do *you* want to do?" I asked.

"I just want to shoot some birds."

"Well, they were supposed to stock some at the state park near the lake. If you just want to shoot birds, not necessarily *wild* birds, we could go there."

"There are probably lots of wild birds there, too. 'Course, it's not like hunting at the *club*," he said sardonically.

(Apparently, I'd been bragging a bit too much lately about our success at the club.)

"You could join, too. And besides, there are native birds there, too."

Brian sniffed distastefully even though by year's end he would be asking for an application. He was right about the state park. The place was known—at least to the area's small fraternity of wild-pheasant hunters—to be crawling with birds all year long, not just during the opening week's stocking. Of course, the population undoubtedly benefited from the introduction of several dozen pen-raised birds, but after all, *none* of the pheasants on our continent are native, the creature having been introduced from China. (I use these rationalizations all the time, so you might as well get used to them.)

Turning the truck toward the lake, I watched the golden field of wild grass disappear in the rear window. Maggie still paced frantically in the back of the truck. When we finally arrived at the park, I was relieved to see only one other truck, so I steered into a small pull-off spot half a mile up the road from it. As the engine died, I spotted a rooster pheasant sitting in the trail thirty yards from us. Wordlessly I pointed it out to Brian.

Thanks to my membership in the hunting club, I already had a good number of pheasants under my belt this year. Brian, on the other hand, had exactly zero. So it didn't surprise me when he leaped from the truck, jammed shells into his autoloader, and raced toward the rooster. The bird watched him coming for all of about a tenth of a second before disappearing into the brush. When it became obvious from my ringside seat that my partner wasn't going to flush it out alone, I pulled on my vest and grabbed my gun before walking around to free Maggie while the bird's scent was still hot. I lowered the tailgate, and the reason for Maggie's agitation during the drive became apparent as the smell of fresh dog excrement all but knocked me over backward.

She looked at me sheepishly as if to say, "I *tried* telling you!"

I found a Burger King napkin and tossed the mess into the nearby brush with unabashed disgust. When I finally caught up with them, Brian was holding his gun at the ready, pointing Maggie to the patch where the bird had last been out in the open. Granted, it was the dry, gravelly ground of an old ATV trail, but I was still surprised when she didn't show the least bit of interest. The bird must have really hightailed it out of there. I can't blame it—if I saw Brian running at me, armed or not, I'd be scared, too.

"So, do you suppose that was one of those tame roosters sitting here waiting for you to come shoot it in broad daylight?" I asked with a good deal of sarcasm.

"Are you ready to hunt or what?" he replied.

Halfway down the trail, we guessed that our chances of spotting another one sitting stupidly out in the open were fairly remote, even if there were stocked birds around. I doubted that, thanks to the several piles of feathers we'd already come across during our brief walk. It seemed that the guys who'd been here this morning had enjoyed a good day.

We broke out into the open fields and spent the next hour and a half watching Maggie get birdy exactly zero times. A faint cackle back toward the trail, followed by a pair of shots and some hollering and dog-whistling, made us angle gently back in that direction, where we bumped into two other guys following a Brittany. Tail feathers poked out of both of their vests. When they turned east, we entered the field and headed northwest, away from them. But they turned suddenly and were cutting in front of us. Assuming their dog was on scent, we backed off and headed in another direction. They cut us off again, making it apparent that this was their field, all two hundred acres of it, and they weren't about to tolerate anyone else in it. Angry, we headed back into the brush. Unbelievably, they cut into the brush and intercepted us again.

Now, I'm not sure if they were rude or just incredibly stupid (the consensus we reached later), but they seemed determined to stay right in front of us. Suddenly I remembered why I detest hunting public land.

I'd been here once last year, with my father. He'd called me, excited that he'd spotted a coyote and a rooster pheasant in the trail, and insisted that I meet him there the next morning. I made a sardonic remark about the bird being a stocker and the coyote being there to make dinner out of him. Nonetheless, Dad was insistent that all we had to do was show up and the birds would be there for the taking. Not viewing the excursion very seriously, I took Ted and rested Maggie, who had flushed over a dozen wild birds the first two days of the season (a far cry from this year). Dad had pointed out where the pheasant had been, and I opined that the bird was most likely basting in coyote stomach acid right now. Indeed, we didn't flush any birds around that spot, or in the same fields that Brian and I were now walking. But on the way out, Ted suddenly dashed off the trail and a bright rooster took to the air about twenty yards to my right. My father, also to my right, had an easy shot. Unfortunately, he saw my fast gun mount and did the only thing that came to mind: Instead of shooting, he ducked. That threw my timing off, and it took both barrels to hit the bird. When Ted finally brought it to my hand, my father was grinning ear to ear.

Yeah, Dad, it's always just that easy.

End of flashback. All of us were suffering in the heat. Brian and I were panting as badly as Maggie, who had covered a lot more ground than we had. I figured that once we hit the trail, we would drop over a steep bank and let Maggie go down to the creek for a drink. As we approached the creek, the ash trees in the foreground stood out pale yellow against the bright orange of the maples and the deep auburn of oaks, all of this against the backdrop of a deep blue sky. *Outdoor Life*, indeed. Then I did a double-take: A patch of white in the crotch of one of the great oaks caught my eye. Maggie was only five yards from the tree and most likely oblivious to the presence of the pheasant when it flew from its roost and into the pattern of birdshot hurled by Brian's Winchester. The bird flopped to the ground and slid down the steep bank to the creek. Maggie, shadowing the bird as it went, dove over the bank with breathtaking speed. In my mind's eye I imagined her lying at the bottom of the steep drop with a broken neck. Instead, I was treated to the sight of my beloved little bird dog doing the canine equivalent of rock climbing with the dead bird in her mouth, grunting like a man as she worked steadily up. Finally reaching the top, she deposited the bird at my feet, spit out some feathers, and disappeared back over the bank. At the creek's edge Maggie drank and drank and drank. And when she began gagging from drinking too fast, she plunged into the wide, blue creek and swam toward the far bank. I'm not sure where she was headed, but at the sound of my whistle, she turned about-face and swam back. She appeared to be smiling as she exited the water far below us and shook herself dry, but she didn't climb the bank quite as quickly the second time. Brian patted her on the head, thanking her for the bird before she dove back into a thorny patch of cover.

We stood with our guns down for a few minutes, waiting while Maggie worked another scent trail.

"Probably a rabbit," I said—just as another ringneck took to the air a few yards in front of me (if it seems that I am wrong a lot, you are right). At my shot, the bird dropped back into a nasty mess of blackberry thorns, and I cringed as Maggie dove in for the retrieve. *I'll be picking thorns out of her hide for hours tonight*, I thought. She dropped the bird at our feet, and Brian and I smiled like mercenaries.

"You know, these *have* to be stocked birds," I said to him.

He didn't say a word.

Forty-five minutes later, Maggie began making game, running better than a hundred yards through thick thorns and tearing brush. She snorted and huffed and kept her nose down, taking a terrible beating from the nagging brush. I resisted the urge this time to comment that it might be another rabbit—I may be wrong a lot, but I learn quickly. When the third rooster went up, I shot and the bird faltered in the air, colliding with some vines hanging from a maple tree. Brian shot, taking it all the way down.

"Why didn't you shoot?" he asked.

"I did!"

"When?"

"I shot first, then you brought it down."

Brian looked at me as if I'd grown a fourth eye. It took us a moment to figure out that we'd shot simultaneously the first time. Laughing, we knew it wasn't the first time that had happened. Maggie brought the bird back and dropped it several yards short of us, in a patch of shade where she could rest. The dog looked positively happy, but absolutely spent.

"We should take her home," I said.

"Let's get her a drink," Brian suggested.

I knew what he was thinking—one more bird and we would have a limit. It happens rarely, and had never happened to him. We all fought the brush down to the creek, Brian and I waiting while Maggie rejuvenated herself with a short drink and a long swim. Back up on the trail, she was still moving slowly, and we reluctantly began working back toward the truck. Without warning, Maggie pounced from the trail back in the direction of the creek. We waited, listening to her disappear in the distance. The wall of thorns she'd gone into was all but impenetrable to humans. So we waited.

When the rooster cackled, Brian and I both gripped the stocks of our guns tightly, knowing that this was going to be it for the day. Either a celebration or another long chase would soon be under way. But as quickly as the flapping and squawking started, it stopped. Then, nothing. Some moments later we could hear Maggie coming slowly through the brush. The rooster had probably run her to the bank, I figured, taking the last bit of her energy before flushing across the creek and into the safety of the private land on the far side.

But then she emerged from the thorny fortress cradling a large, dead rooster pheasant in her mouth. Dropping it at Brian's feet, she shook herself off and turned for the truck without so much as a wag of her tired tail.

Brian and I stood there dumbfounded before high-fiving and breaking into a gale of laughter.

"Two for me, one for you, and one for Mag . . . *limit!*"

Later that night, the excitement faded to some extent with the knowledge that those had most likely been stocked birds. For today, the celebration was sincere, but tomorrow. . . .

Wild birds, wild birds, wild birds.

Thursday

I awoke with one thought this morning: *wild birds.*

I love to take pictures and have ever since I was eleven or twelve. Recently I bought a couple of good Nikon cameras with the rationale that the photos would help me sell magazine articles. Unfortunately, the money I've made from the sale of a handful of pictures is only about enough to supply the cameras with batteries every other time they need them. I don't really mind, though, since the pictures are really for me. Sure, sometimes I sell them and often I bring them to work to show them off, but mostly they are tucked away in the albums that I restlessly page through in the odd months when there isn't some kind of critter to hunt. Those pictures are often a source of comfort, reminding me that hunting season isn't all that far away.

Much like my philosophy about hunting (if there's a season open, carry a gun; if that gun can hold eighty shells, load it fully), I adhere to a general rule of photography, too: *If you're going afield, carry a camera!* Yes, it gets tiresome having those heavy cameras banging against your chest when you're sprinting downfield after a running rooster. Yes, the camera often stays in its case for three or four trips in a row, and thus I've done nothing more than lug around five extra pounds of useless weight along with my gun and vest full of goodies. There hasn't been a day when I've regretted bringing it along, but there have been several when I've deeply regretted leaving it at home or, worse, back in the truck, just out of reach. This was destined to be one of those days.

Still depressed over our lack of success on wild ringnecks, I felt almost ready to hang it up and just hunt woodcock. Yet I had the day to myself and was not giving up. It promised to be another dark, damp one, but surprisingly, my bird-hunting spirit was not yet completely broken, thanks probably to the vests full of birds—stocked or not—that Brian and I had brought home last night. The ground was still dry when my alarm went off, but the brooding skies were full of evil intent. Though I was in the mood to hunt— I hadn't taken these weeks of vacation for nothing, after all—I wasn't in the mood to get soaked alone.

Like misery, birdhunters love company.

My father hadn't been out with me for a while, so I gave him a call. He's usually good for three or four hunts a year with me, and I was hoping this would be one of them. I was pleased when he agreed, though I lied just a bit about what I thought the weather would be like: "Cloudy? Rain? I haven't heard the forecast, Dad." In his driveway, he cast a wary glance at the advancing band of black sky. I shrugged. My father, however, is a smart man, and tucked under his right arm was a rolled-up vinyl raincoat.

I hadn't yet tried two of my several places to hunt wild pheasants, but the inexplicable need to hunt Betty's field once again drew me there. Three damp, birdless, raccoon-infested trips to the spot hadn't erased the vision of those two big roosters the dogs and I scared up back during our early-season scouting mission. Those pheasants had to be there still—just had to be.

Wading into the mess of wild grass and dogwood, I felt the familiar lift of the cool north breeze. For the first time this year, the brush wasn't wet, but crisp and dry instead, thanks to that same north wind that had blown steadily all night. I was glad not to be soaked to my Fruit-of-the-Looms, but knew that an overnight wind almost always meant rain. The advancing blackness did nothing to change my suspicion.

Not thinking, I had put both dogs in the truck. Now I was sorry I'd brought Ted along. His eye was more clouded than before and had begun oozing. I peeled back his eyelid for a close look and finally spotted the minute scratch on the lens. Calling Greta on the cell phone, I asked her to make an appointment at the vet for him. She called back to confirm a visit for this afternoon. Oh, well, by the looks of it we'd be rained out by then, and if I scoured this field for a third time without so much as a hen flush, I'd be seriously considering getting out of the pheasant-hunting business, at least for a while. I knew my ardor couldn't withstand many more fruitless hours in this field.

Following the familiar course to the back of the field, we zigzagged a couple of times through the miniponds. I watched carefully for snipe, but none flew out of the puddles with that odd towering flush I had hoped to show my dad. No snipe, no rabbits, no pheasants—not even the odd killer raccoon to liven things up.

Once we'd investigated the majority of the cover the field had to offer, I guessed it wouldn't hurt to try those God-awful ruts. If I was a pheasant and knew a nasty storm was approaching, I might be tempted to hunker down under a piece of brush in the deep ruts and wait it out. I have no idea if that's how pheasants think, but it seemed at least to give us a focal point for our energy on this otherwise unrewarding morning. Instead of hiking directly to the rutted field, I decided to go by way of one of the sparser fields that we had tried on opening day, just to change things up a bit. Pheasants, like all game animals, are aware of the movement patterns of predators around them, and since we'd tried that very approach several times now, I thought mixing things up a bit might do us some good. To my surprise, the corner of one of those sparse fields we'd barely touched held some good, chest-high cover. I couldn't identify the grass or weed, but it was brittle and bushy and gray, and though it was hell to walk through, the dogs navigated effortlessly under the canopy and so, I reasoned, would the pheasants.

A shot, finally!

Just as we began wading into the unusual brush, a narrow band of sun broke out low on the eastern horizon, illuminating the underside of the black clouds. My dad and the dogs were bathed in supernatural orange light against the gray brush and the black sky. This was the kind of picture you saw in magazines. A surefire winner. Instinctively, I reached for the camera pack, realizing immediately that I'd left it back in the truck, worried that the rain would damage it.

It never fails.

Although I didn't voice my anger to my father, I was frustrated as we plodded into the field, delicate branches cracking under the fiery glow bathing the belly of the black clouds. We worked the small, dense patch of cover in circles, and I was disappointed, yet far from surprised, when the dogs didn't pick up any scent. I could see that Ted was favoring his eye and trying not to touch the brush with it. *I should take him back to the truck,* I thought as we broke out of the odd cover and into the rutted field. I certainly wouldn't be heartbroken—nor would Dad—to miss the big field's angry ruts with their hip-grinding and ankle-twisting properties.

Before I could ask my dad's take on the situation, a loud cackling from Betty's field riveted our attention. Amazed, we watched a rooster pheasant launch from the hedgerow I'd elected not to push through for the sake of variety (*Smart, Joel, simply brilliant*). I figured the rooster had probably waited until we were well past before showing itself and was now destined to soar away to the far cornfield. So I couldn't believe it when it began flying *toward* us. Silhouetted against the black sky and bathed in orange light, the cockbird was a breathtaking sight.

"Don't move, Dad. Maggie, Ted, *stay!*"

Like four odd statues, we stood at the edge of the gray cover and watched the bird lock his wings and— *Oh, thank you, Lord!*—coast into the odd gray cover we'd just left. He flared and touched down less than a hundred yards away. Fortunately, the dogs were out of the bird's line of sight or they would have gone after it, no questions asked. I could see Dad looking at me as I tried to mark a reference point in the cover where the bird went in. I held up my hand to shush him for a minute as I picked out a red oak tree in a far hedgerow for a landmark. It was a good plan if the bird was just coming into the cover to roost, but if he had spotted us on his incoming flight, he could just as well hit the ground running—probably in the opposite direction.

We gave the bird a moment or two to settle in, then slowly began working back into the crackling gray ground cover, trying with great difficulty to move quietly. If the bird hadn't spotted us on the way into the field, it would be a miracle if he didn't hear us coming. I kept the oak tree in my line of sight, and as we neared the spot where I was sure the bird had landed, I pointed to the ground to tell Dad *right here.* He held his shotgun at the ready, almost comically. If anyone looked primed to miss a bird, it was he— there is such a thing as being *too ready,* and he was the poster boy for that condition. We walked gingerly the last few steps before breaking out onto the tractor path, now beyond the cover.

"Where did he go?" Dad asked.

"He probably heard us coming and hit the open path running."

Dad looked glum. It isn't often that a rooster virtually flies into your lap around here, and though Dad is not an avid bird hunter, it was not lost on him that we seemed to have blown that one-in-a-thousand chance to pieces. As the sun began melting back into its gray shroud, it appeared that this would be a day chock-full of missed opportunities. Maggie and Ted sniffed around restlessly on the tractor path, scenting nothing. I thought they might pick up the scent of the bird exiting the cover and at least give him a run down the tractor path, but they didn't come up with anything. I took the dogs around to the back of the field, where the tractor path cut ninety degrees to the right, to see if the bird had slipped out that way, but again they picked up nothing. I began pondering. Either the bird had sneaked back between us—unlikely in this narrow patch of cover—or it had simply sat tight and let the wind carry its scent away. Dry days like that do not make for good ground scenting. Perhaps the dogs had run right past the bird, sensing my excitement and working a bit too fast. *Let's try something else,* I thought to myself.

Remembering how the dogs had puttered around and sniffed at scent while we stood in the tractor path talking, I knew that's exactly the slow, methodical, casual kind of work they would have to do to root this bird out of the cover—provided he was still there.

I motioned for Dad to follow me, and we stepped back into the same cover we'd just come out of. Then I gestured for him to stop. We stood there as the dogs worked out ahead of us, quartering and sniffing and slowly getting a bit too far out. When Ted realized we were fifty yards away, he trotted happily back. Maggie wasn't far behind. As we waited, the dogs looked at us briefly to see which direction we were heading, and when they realized we weren't heading anywhere, they began sniffing and puttering, working a slow circle around us without going anywhere. *Perfect.* Dad had a slightly bored look on his face. The poster boy for

Ted taking a well-deserved break.

too ready now looked a bit weary—of course, that's when the rooster came up in front of him. My father was to my left, and the bird came up between us and swung left in front of him. Reflexively, my gun came up to back him, but he did the unexpected once again: He ducked. In a hail of unprintable words and lead— both mine—Thursday's Bird came crashing down to Ted's great black, waiting jaws.

I glared at my father, who immediately voiced his fear of my mistakenly shooting him when he saw my gun come up so fast. I rolled my eyes as we tucked the first wild bird of the season into my game vest.

All that really mattered was that we had grounded a wild ringneck after three long, hard days and part of a fourth.

After cleaning up the yellow puddle Ted left in the entryway to the vet's office—his little vote of protest and one which Greta and I and the vet have all gotten used to—we settled in as best we could in the waiting room. There was no calming Ted, who, though normally very agreeable, really hates the vet. I couldn't blame him. Two of his trips there involved the exact same freak accident: He caught his toenail in the runner of our sliding glass door, cracking it in one instance and nearly amputating it in the other. Both outings to the vet involved removing the nail and exposing the nerve, an experience that would certainly make me do battle with anyone who tried to drag me back to that same doctor again. Though the last of the nail injuries had happened over a year ago, Ted's memories of the painful incident still remained as we walked into the vet's waiting room. That is to say, he was simply insane.

By the time the vet's assistant led us into the examining room, Ted was beside himself with terror, having left a trickling yellow trail into the small white room. Ken, the assistant, is an avid hunter and a big fan of Ted and Maggie, and when he caught Ted's big black head between his hands, the look on his face was one of genuine concern. I was worried, too. The dog's eye had gone from a gauzy gray to complete cloudiness in just the past few hours. When I saw the concern on Ken's face, my own got worse.

"What happened?"

"It looks like a scratch in the top of the eye," I said, trying to hide my nervousness.

Ken nodded, prying the eyelids apart and seeing the small red streak in the cloudy glass at the top of the pupil.

"These hunting dogs . . . you never know what they're going to get into, isn't that right, Teddy?" he said, ruffling the big dog's ears.

It did little to calm Ted down. Though he might like Ken—he likes everyone—I'm sure he associated him only with the most painful times in his life. Although Ted would never hurt a flea, I thought Ken had a lot of nerve to put his face down by those jaws.

When the vet came in, a neat young man whom I didn't recall ever meeting before, the same look of concern furrowed his brow. My heart began beating harder.

"How long ago did this happen?"

I didn't like the tone already.

"A day or two ago," I said nervously.

"And you're just bringing him in today?"

He was undoubtedly accusing me.

"Every night after we hunt, I clean the dog's eyes out. I thought he must have gotten a scratch . . . I didn't think . . . It just got cloudy today. . . ."

"*Hmm*," the vet said, turning his attention back to the dog.

I wanted to yell, *Hey, you dummy, these dogs are not abused hunting dogs—they sleep at the foot of my bed, they play with my kids, they watch TV with me on the couch, for heaven's sake. I cook them scrambled eggs for breakfast! I love my dogs!*

But I stayed quiet, and thankfully, the scolding stopped.

While Ken applied some anesthetic to the eyeball, the vet rolled in a blacklight examination lamp with a large magnifying glass on an arm. As concerned as I was about my dog, I couldn't help wondering what it would cost to flick the switch on this glorified desk lamp (forty-five bucks). As I held Ted's quivering paws, the vet, bending over the light, now positioned above Ted's head, took the dog's head in his hands and peeled back the eyelids. Unlike when Ken had done it, Ted didn't wince. The anesthetic must have been working. With a couple more protracted "*Hmmms*" and "*Ahh-hahs*," the vet slid back and motioned me over to the light.

"Look at your *scratch*, Joel."

With more than a little trepidation, I slid onto the tall stool and looked down while the vet held Ted's head in the correct position. Once my eyes adjusted to the odd black light and the thick focus of the magnifier, I found myself looking at a river-sized red gouge ending in a tiny piece of thorn. The point of the thorn—nearly microscopic—pierced deeply into the smooth glass of Ted's eye.

"Crap," I said involuntarily.

"*Deep* crap, if you'd have let that stay there. As it is, that's going to take a while to heal, once we get it out," the vet said, his voice somewhat less accusatory, though still holding an edge.

I love my dogs! I love my dogs!!!

With a pair of fine tweezers, the vet expertly extracted the thorn and placed it on a piece of gauze, where it was barely visible. He motioned me over to the lamp again, and I saw the hole, which, at whatever magnification that thing operates, looked like you could drive a truck into it. Once the room lights were back on and the lamp off, the nick in the eye was barely visible.

"Do you have other dogs?" the vet asked.

Ken smiled behind the new vet.

"Yes." *Are you going to call the SPCA on me?*

"Good, because old Ted won't be hunting for a week."

Whew. I could keep Maggie.

"Will the cloudiness go away?" I asked, still worried.

"Yeah, that's just a result of the trauma. It will dissipate. But one of the creams I'll give you will keep it dilated, so he can't go out in the sunshine."

No more traumatizing your dog, you abusive bastard.

We left, sixty bucks poorer and two tiny little tubes of eye cream richer. Ted couldn't get in the truck fast enough. Me either.

CHAPTER FOUR

DIGGING IN

Saturday

There's something about a foggy morning. Having risen before the sun for the past five days, I really didn't relish the thought of getting up early again. But it was Saturday, the day I'd promised to take out my older daughter Jessica as well as my brother-in-law Steve and Eric, my nephew. I had no doubt that the kids would do well—both Eric and Jessica are active and pack energy enough to power several adults with several million kilowatts left over. Just my excitement was lacking.

Steve hadn't been out yet, but I'd told him stories of our wild days of woodcock shooting, and he was eager to go. He mentioned that he'd never shot a pheasant and was excited about that, too, but given the events of the past few days, I didn't want to encourage that line of thinking. (*In fact*, I thought, *if Steve ends up popping a wild rooster after I hunted the whole week's worth of vacation with exactly one bird to show for it, I believe I will cry.*) Even John had called me yesterday, anxious to get out with Minnie, his new yellow Lab.

I made plans, kept my promises, but didn't really have the heart for it. To relieve the stress of visiting the vet, I'd gone out just before dark yesterday to hunt deer from my bow stand, but save for the frontal assault of an angry red squirrel, it did nothing to prime me for another day of hunting. If it hadn't been for the kids, I probably would have backed out.

But something happened on the way to the field, as they say. There was something captivating about the dense fog hanging over the fields and the way the orange treetops poked through it. It was warm, but not *too* warm. Here and there, hints of the brilliant blue October sky peeked through the fog, promising a good backdrop for the day's hunt once the fog burned off or blew away. So I did something I hadn't done for a couple days: I let myself get hopeful.

Once out of the truck, we herded the kids and the dogs away from the road, since the fog was so thick that oncoming cars might not be able to see my parked truck until they were on top of it. In fact, that unpleasant possibility motivated me to move the truck

Taking the kids into woodcock cover.

farther over until it teetered dangerously near the edge of a ditch.

With the kids in oversized orange vests and sweatshirts, we moved out. Our little safari consisted of three hunters, two kids, and two dogs—one lame (Maggie) and one a puppy that seemed to delight in jumping on the lame one. I'd taken Maggie over to the ditch across the road and run her a bit to see if she looked able to handle a day's hunt. She didn't show even the slightest gimp then, but now I suspected she had been acting.

We kept the kids behind us, and I let John and Steve work slightly ahead of me. Maggie glanced through them to me in the odd moments when she paid attention to my hand signals, but in true Maggie fashion, she didn't really care who was carrying the guns at the ready. She was there to hunt. Once she began probing the brush and deep grass, all traces of her stiffness were gone. Minnie bounded merrily along behind her but quickly decided it was more fun to hang out with the kids, who showered her with nonstop attention. John tried encouraging the puppy to get out and hunt a little more actively, but the kids proved too much of a distraction.

Once again we worked to the back of the field with nothing to show for it. No one looked quite as disappointed as I felt. Where the field broke into saplings—among which we'd killed the first woodcock on opening day this year—we headed into them instead of back around the other side of the field. I switched the sixes in my side-by-side for the eights I'd brought. I wanted the kids to see some action.

It didn't take long. The first woodcock came up between John and Steve, and their guns cracked nearly simultaneously. The bird fell, and Maggie delivered it to Steve, who was delighted at his first woodcock. I turned and asked the kids what they thought about that. Killing is not always something that is easy to witness, even for kids from hunting families.

"Cool!" was the joint pronouncement of the cousins.

Right answer.

A narrow drainage ditch bisected the small patch of beech slash. Once we hit that, we turned to work along the length of the ditch, and I got ready. A woodcock burst from the little ditch with a harsh peep and a mad fluttering of wings. I couldn't believe it when I missed with both shots. Steve tried backing me up and missed it as well. We marked the place where the bird dropped back into the cover not far ahead of us and went after it. On the way I heard a loud "*sqauwww*" overhead and glanced up in time to see a crow appear low over the trees and flare, suddenly realizing his mistake. My shot was instinctive, and the crow whistled down like an errant bomb, loudly crashing to the ground right at the feet of Eric and Jessica.

"Awesome!"

I would take these two hunting anytime.

When we finally hit the spot where we'd marked the woodcock, a tiny finger of dogwood poking out into the field, we were all ready. I motioned the kids to stay well back as John and Steve and I covered the three sides of the bush. The bird went out across in front of me. I should have had him on the first shot but apparently had accidentally loaded blanks. The bird whizzed past John, who took it on his third shot. The volley was deafening in the quiet confines of the foggy thicket.

Don't drop that woodcock!

Eric and Jessica were smiling from ear to ear. "Wow!"

Seeing their enthusiasm for our hunting stirred my own and enlivened my tired carcass, and I almost didn't care if we didn't get any pheasants. We killed one more woodcock in the slash before heading back out to the open fields in earnest search of pheasants. Reloading with sixes (which I cautiously shook to make sure *they* weren't blanks), I led the party along the back edge of the field to the narrow patch of odd gray cover where Thursday's Bird had finally offered itself up, hoping to repeat the performance. Then we crossed the field again, pushed through the dogwoods, and then slowly crossed the ruts to the big cornfield on the opposite side.

We followed two of the small drainages through the corn. I hung back with the kids and listened intently to Maggie racing impetuously through the corn. I wouldn't have been surprised to see or hear a rooster go up, but I doubted that it would be anywhere near us. The birds would run the dogs all day in that corn. Even Minnie, despite her puppy energy, quickly tired of the long yellow rows, leaving Maggie to work alone, the way she likes it. I could make out snippets of corn rows being parted and hear the tinkling of her collar tags, but for the most part I had no clue where Maggie was and just prayed she was somehow paralleling our progress. When she finally appeared to our left, Maggie had her nose down, and I think she was as surprised as I to find she was so close to us. There was no doubt that she was working scent. She followed the trail through the last few rows of corn and out into another small patch of dogwoods at the south end of the field. We'd killed several roosters there over the years, so I quickly followed. This was just the kind of thing a wild bird would do, run the dog up one row and down another, then cut across the whole field to escape into a patch of heavy cover, perhaps flushing wild if the dog was dedicated enough to keep up pursuit.

This dog was.

With the speed Maggie was moving ahead of me and from what little I could glimpse, I expected the flush at any moment. I knew it was going to be a rooster and was dimly aware of the rest of our hunting party coming up behind me, Steve leading them. When the sound of panicked wingbeats came from the dogwoods ten yards in front of us, my gun came up. As the bird emerged into the foggy morning air, I slid off my safety. I heard Steve's safety click off, too, as his gun swung quickly up alongside mine. It was all I could do to get the word out.

"Hen!"

Steve still held his shotgun up as if he was going to shoot. He looked across the stock at me, questioning.

"Hen?"

I nodded my head, and his gun lowered slowly.

"Oh."

"Yeah. I would have bet money it was. . . ."

"Why didn't you shoot?" Eric asked.

"It was a female," Jessica said. "And you can't kill them. You can only shoot males. *Roosters.*"

That's my kid.

"Oh," Eric said, his disappointment mirroring his father's.

"What did you guys think about that?" I asked.

"I wish it was a rooster," Eric said.

I'll take those two kids hunting anytime.

Permission

There is only so much you can do when the day goes kaput. Poking and prodding every inch of cover for the past five hours, we hadn't so much as flushed a cottontail. I was exasperated. Brian was quiet. Maggie was dragging herself along, exhibiting none of the enthusiasm she'd had at noon yesterday. With Ted gone, she had hunted twice as hard, perhaps sensing that she must, but she was beginning to suffer the effects of a hard week's hunting. Unbelievably, we had only one wild pheasant and one wounded dog to show for it.

Halfway back to the truck, the chat that bounced occasionally between Brian and me related mostly to what we could and should be getting done this afternoon. Though the weather was the best it had been yet—dry and about 45 degrees, nearly perfect— we simply didn't have much desire to go on. It had been a slow morning. At least when you flush a hen or the dogs put up turkeys or snipe or woodcock or whatever—*anything*—you get a little visual stimulation. Today we'd seen nothing but the tops of our boots and Maggie's brown-and-white back. In the fourth hour of the hunt, even she showed signs of holding out little hope for a flush. By the end of the fifth, she was just walking along with us. Wherever the critters were today, they certainly weren't here.

I thought about taking a long break through midday, but when Maggie needed to be lifted into the truck, I knew we wouldn't be coming back out this evening. The dog, like her master, needed a break. With the cool weather, it would be a good night to sit up in one of my bowhunting stands. The deer should be moving on a day like this. After the fruitless morning, my mind drifted easily away from the birds.

We sat on the tailgate while Maggie gulped water and collapsed—but gingerly—in a heap on her old blue blanket. Folding one leg at a time under herself, she let one—the left front—stick oddly out in front of her and immediately began licking it. Brian and I agreed it was time to hang it up.

Still sitting on the tailgate and running my hand over Maggie, I watched Brian drive off. She'd picked up an amazing assortment of stickers and burrs, even though we'd given her fringes a "sport cut" just before the season. My hand would travel only an inch before a hard knot or a burr stopped it. Equally amazing was the number of thorns poking into her pink hide. Some of them were nasty half-inch long thornapple spikes poking all the way into her save for a tiny, hard lump where the base protruded. Maggie's sides shuddered and she occasionally flinched as I removed the often bloody thorns, but she never complained, just glad to be rid of them. The burrs took more coaxing, but with a little work they, too, came out of her silky fur. As the pile of vegetation on the tailgate grew bigger and bigger, it wasn't the burrs that worried me. It was Maggie's leg. I hoped she would be all right. With Ted out of commission, I didn't have another backup dog, and I certainly didn't want to hurt Maggie. It began to look more and more like this week's vacation would focus on bowhunting instead of birdhunting. I love to hunt deer, but this was still very early in the season. Besides, I had weeks set aside for that game later in the year, and I really wanted to get some more wild birds.

By the time the last of the thorns and stickers were yanked from her brown-and-white fur, Maggie was snoring. That she could sleep through someone pulling and plucking painfully at her skin was testament to how tired she really was. Closing the tailgate, then the cap, I walked—pretty stiffly myself— around to the front of the truck and climbed in. I was about to turn the key when something caught my eye. A small piece of paper was flapping under my windshield wiper. I rolled down the window, reached around, and snatched it up.

In neat, small script, the note said: "I think you are a bit confused about where you are allowed to hunt."

Angry, I glared up and down the road at the half-dozen houses within sight. Granted, I was on private land—all three of the properties we'd hunted across today were posted—but I had meticulously secured permission on each of them this past year.

Two of the property owners I've known since childhood, and the last I'd introduced myself to this summer, though "introduced" doesn't quite fit since he probably thought I was stalking him. Five times in seven days I'd cruised slowly by his barn, hoping to spot him working there or in the fields. It didn't happen, so I kept riding by, watching and hoping.

Then I finally hit it right.

It all started with the tragic loss of my eighty-two-acre plot last summer, over which I was still in mild shock. Trying to stem my anger at the thoughtless landowner's planned use and abuse of what once was prime bird habitat, I had set out to find more places to hunt.

Driving home from work one day, mildly depressed after passing my mourned hunting spot, I'd had an idea. I turned down one of the back roads, planning just to cruise until I came upon the first likely looking patch of pheasant cover. Then I would ask permission. Right then. No waiting. I drove north toward Lake Ontario and didn't find one open grass field. There was young corn, young beans, tomatoes,

Working the grass fields.

and countless other crops but no long-grass cover and no hedgerows. Turning down the next road, I found the same thing. Next road, same thing. Over and over. One turn finally put me in a block of good cover. It was one I already had permission to hunt, but I'd never seen a bird there. Like John's sister-in-law's place, it was just one more in a long string of good-looking bird covers with no birds.

Heading back toward my hometown of Ransomville, I had passed the tiny hospital where I was born, now a nursing home, passed the church where I was baptized, and the house in which I grew up. I drove by my best friend's former house (he's now in Arizona), the town bully's house (he's now in jail), my grandmother's house (she's still there), and a dozen other places where I'd laughed and cried and played and fought. The town whizzed by, and I soon found myself back out in the country again. Slowing and stopping next to a long-grass field, I leaned out the window and said hello to an elderly woman working in her garden.

Thankfully, permission came easily that time.

Several days last year, Maggie and Ted and I had trod across the rutted, overgrown farm fields there. The walking was pure hell, but we rarely left the place without a pheasant in the game bag. We often hunted the entire property, stopping only at the neighbor's heavily posted fenceline. "Warning!" the sign read, "Trespassers Will Be Prosecuted." The only trespasser last year was Ted, who dutifully trotted after a rooster I hit that had rainbowed gracefully over the line, landing twenty yards into the lovely long grass of the posted land. He was hesitant about going over for the retrieve, so I lied, assuring him we had a good lawyer.

After hunting that property, we often drove a short distance up the road to another tract of land on which I had secured permission. Hunting that place one day, I realized it ended on the opposite side of the heavily posted property we butted up against at the other place. Several roosters we chased out of the cornfield landed safely on the posted land, untouchable to man and dog alike. If I could get permission on the center piece of grassland, we'd have a huge, unbroken area to hunt. But the line of angry red "Warning!" signs convinced me to let the subject drop. Pheasant season came and went, and I never thought about the property again—until I lost my favorite place (have I mentioned the eighty-two acres . . . how nice it was?). Then my mind turned back to the center section missing from my hunting domain, the red-signed no-man's-land where the birds grew wild and old on berry bushes and cornfields, their great, droopy tail feathers hidden in the long, golden grass.

So I began stalking the farmer—I guess there's no other way to put it.

I don't particularly like introducing myself to strangers, but when it comes to securing hunting land, I become reasonably outgoing. I've dealt with farmers all my life, and have set some fairly strict guidelines when asking them for hunting permission:

1. Don't stop during the harvest season or any other time they're busy. If they are picking or combining or spraying or haying, they are damn busy and don't have the time or patience to deal with some namby-pamby hunter worried about finding a place to exercise his dogs.

2. Don't dress fancy. Jehovah's Witnesses dress fancy.
   Enough said.
3. Drive the vehicle you are going to have during
   hunting season. If the farmer has seen your truck
   before, you are a lot less likely to find it flattened by
   a hundred-ton combine if you park in the wrong spot.
4. Don't say a lot. Ask; then shut up.
5. Don't go to the door—you'll seem like a salesman or
   a Jehovah's Witness (albeit a mangy one, if you
   follow Rule Number 2). Try to find him outside,
   but make sure he's not busy, or doing something
   you are neither talented nor motivated enough to
   help with.
6. If he says no, don't cry—not in front of him, anyway.

After carefully watching the posted property for the
better part of a week, I finally spotted the farmer next
to the barn, but he was lodged under his tractor and I
could clearly see the metallic shine of a crescent
wrench in his hand. I'm of little value when it comes
to anything more mechanical than breaking open a
shotgun to stuff in another shell, so I sped off. The
next day, I again came home from work via the hunting
area and applauded my luck when I saw him pulling
up his driveway in his old pickup. I swung in behind
him, parking my truck right behind his. He eyed me
warily in the rearview before stepping cautiously out
into the drive.

"Help ya?"

Introducing myself, I got right to the point.

"Yep. I've seen ya. You have a Lab and a springer.
Hunt Betty's property."

We're filing suit against your black Lab for
trespassing even as we speak.

"That's right."

"They any good?"

"Yep," I said, observing Rule Number 4.

"You can hunt all you want. Just don't shoot near the house 'n barn."

"Thanks," I said, again shaking his hand. "And that's my truck, in case you see it parked out here."

"Kinda figured it was yours," he said, smiling.

Before I climbed in my truck, I sensed him watching me and turned. He seemed about to say something else, so I rebroke the ice and said, "Thanks, again."

Nodding and smiling, he said, "If you're out here alone, would you mind coming to get me? I have a shotgun or two lying around. Haven't shot a pheasant in years."

"You bet. I've got a question for you, too."

"Shoot."

"Why is the land posted so heavily? Doesn't seem like you're the type to mind folks hunting."

"I don't. I put those signs up a couple years ago because some deer hunters tromped through my parents' backyard. Upset the hell out of Mom. I figured the signs would make folks stop in and introduce themselves and ask. But nobody ever asks."

"Never?"

"Been two years, and you're the first."

I liked the guy, and had felt bad to be the first representative of the hunting fraternity to stop in and ask—though I know damn well that I wasn't the first hunter to set foot on the place in these last couple of years. I'd seen guys hunting it regularly, just last year. Even so, I know it wasn't this farmer who had left me the anonymous note. It just wasn't his style, or his inclination. Angling my truck toward his house, not stalking him but taking the direct approach this time, I sadly thought to myself, *This just isn't getting any easier.*

Determination

Sixes or eights? Pheasants or woodcock?

OK, the pheasants were going to get a break today. Or rather, I suppose, I was going to take a break from letting them get the best of me. When Dad showed up in the driveway, I was still balancing two boxes of shells, one in each hand, like an admittedly unattractive version of Lady Justice.

Sixes or eights? Pheasants or woodcock?

As Dad pulled on his hunting clothes and set his gun in my truck, I set Maggie loose from the house. Though the sun was shining, my stone driveway was muddy and damp, and when she jumped on Dad, pawing at him excitedly, she left muddy tracks from his ankles to his waist. She was ready to go. From just inside the kitchen door, a tortured wail arose unlike anything I had ever heard from Ted. Standing in the picture window in full view of our preparations, he tilted his head back and let out another pathetic wail. I had been locking him in the bedroom as we got ready to go out the last couple of days, but today Greta wasn't home and I didn't want him to be shut in the small room all morning. Chances are that he would pull the down stuffing from our pillows just to have some kind of interaction, however indirect, with birds. Lowering the tailgate to let Maggie in the truck before she further mauled my father, I went back to the house, thinking I'd put the baby gate up in the kitchen and leave Ted there, where at least he'd have a little room to stretch his legs, yet couldn't see us go.

As I walked up the driveway, though, Ted set up his ambush. Figuring he was still in the living room, I opened the door and was promptly flattened by a large black mass moving at an incredible speed. Picking myself up and reattaching my left arm (the one that had been gripping the door), I hollered for Ted, who by then was nowhere in sight.

"He's in with Maggie," Dad said.

Rounding the tailgate of my truck, I found Maggie curled up on her blue blanket. Ted stood all the way to the front of the truck, out of my reach.

"Come, Ted."

His tail wagged just before he lay down.

"Come here."

Nope.

"You better come here . . . *now.*"

Slinking to the tailgate, Ted looked miserably guilty in a way only Labs can. His tail was threaded between his legs and rubbed his belly. Somehow, it was still wagging. In the sunlight I took Ted's head in my hand and turned the big black block this way and that. The cloudiness was gone. Peeling back his eyelid, I looked for the hole but couldn't find it, although there was a tiny red streak where the scratch had been. Sighing, giving up, I said, "Do you want to get some birds?"

Rebounding off my chest with both paws and sending me sprawling for the second time in five minutes, Ted jumped out of the truck and ran fully around it, finally jumping back in with blinding speed. How can you argue with that kind of enthusiasm? (Of course, somewhere in the back of my mind, the new vet's voice was asking, *What's the date? Has it been a week yet? Well, has it?*)

Oh, shut up.

At the field, I loaded up the No. 8 shotshells and zipped up my hunting vest. The day was cloudless and deep blue, and the sun shone fiercely. When Dad was loaded and ready, I opened the tailgate, and the hunting team of Maggie and Ted was complete once again.

Now, I'm not sure how much dogs know, but I am willing to give them a lot of credit for smarts. I think that they probably know when we are going for rabbits as opposed to birds, and they seem to be startlingly aware of the difference between the two words. But when it comes to woodcock versus pheasants, I'm not so sure. Certainly they know that one is feisty and fast and runs like a cheetah, and the other one is small

A nice wild rooster — in woodcock cover!

and spooky and tastes awful, but whether they understand which one we are going after on a given day is open for debate. Most of the woodcock we've shot were taken during pheasant season, and a game bag with a good mix of both birds (and a rabbit or two tossed in for good measure) is not a rarity. So when I set the dogs free from the back of the truck and into one of my favorite patches of woodcock cover, even though it was the middle of wild-pheasant season, I really didn't know what they were thinking. Were they disappointed that we weren't chasing roosters?

According to Maggie, it would seem they were.

About eighty yards from the road she picked up scent, as did Ted. Ready for a flush, we waited and waited. Finally, the dogs took off on a perpendicular line. It definitely wasn't a woodcock. I sighed, knowing that if it was one of the hundreds of rabbits that called the thicket home, I really shouldn't be shooting them with No. 8 shot, unless they were fairly close. And to *not* shoot them would ensure a cross-country chase until the critter holed up. Then the dogs made another hard turn, Ted only inches behind Maggie but with his own nose to the ground and working furiously, and disappeared into a half-acre of dogwoods.

"Rabbit," I said to Dad.

When the rooster came up, I watched it go for a split-second as if I was a spectator at someone else's game. Ted came up underneath it, at least five feet off the ground. When the bird finally got its wings under control and decided which way to fly, my trance was broken. I followed its progress over the fat barrels of my 12-gauge, thinking about the No. 8 shot and wondering if it would do the trick. I shot before the bird could get far enough out to make the call even more questionable. After I found the second trigger, the bird tumbled in the air, but righted itself only two feet above the ground. Locking its wings, it made a hard landing into a small patch of maple saplings. The dogs didn't see the flight of the bird and looked at me, waiting for a hand signal for the retrieve. When it didn't come, they began sniffing madly around our feet, trying to beat each other to the retrieve. At least momentarily, I was glad they were distracted.

"It's going to hit the ground running," I said, stuffing into the Stoeger the two heavy-duty sixes I'd stowed away in my vest.

Nodding, Dad pointed to the spot where the bird had gone down. We began walking that way, and the dogs still acted confused, sniffing around behind us. I didn't want to tell them to "Go fetch it up" because chances were they would flush it wild on us before we could get into range. I didn't want to send them out ahead too far,

Maggie, Ted, and the author.

in case they might pick up the scent. I'm fairly convinced they can even pick up bird smell from the scent trail it leaves flying in the air (call me crazy, but I've . . . well, just call me crazy).

So we let the dogs mistakenly search behind us until we got up into the area where the bird went down. Then I yelled.

"Right here! Right here! Fetch him up!"

The dogs were a blur coming down the field at us, brush snapping and parting in their wake. They sniffed hard, working every inch of brush in a thirty-yard circle. But once the excitement of my exhortation had worn off, they slowed down, finally stopping and looking back at me for a signal.

"Get him!"

They walked back into the cover this time—not even *trotting*—and came back out a moment later. I was dumbfounded.

"Maybe he picked right back up after you saw him lock," I suggested to my dad before he cut me off with a shake of his head.

"He's right here."

"Where?"

"Right by my feet in the trail."

"Grab him."

"He's *alive.*"

"He's a bird. Grab him!"

With a sour look, Dad reached into the brush, but the bird flushed again and once again I tumbled him with the second shot, this time forever. Ted carried the bird part of the way back, then stopped in the trail with it, perhaps thirty yards away.

"Good boy. Come on," I said while I knelt and held out my right hand.

His tail wagged and I swear there was an evil gleam in his eye.

"Ted, now."

The tail kept wagging.

Finally, on some unseen dog-cue, he picked the bird up and trotted to me with it, happily putting it in my hand.

"What's gotten into you? Are you mad at me because you had to stay home this week?"

More wagging.

Enter Mr. Murphy

It was time to go after the rooster behind the house again. The thought of that bird sitting back there so close to the house had haunted me for days. Now, with Brian once again with me, I was ready.

Approaching the hedgerow, I held Maggie at a careful heel (not an easy task for either Maggie or me). With the memory of the escaped wild bird fresh in my mind, I had devised a plan while lying in bed last night. Yes, it had come to this: I was treating a pheasant like a trophy big-game animal for which "plans" and "schemes" were needed to get a whack at it. As always, we were willing to try whatever might work, and I was quite confident this indeed might work if the bird was still around. Since Maggie was more resistant to heeling than usual—even whimpering in protest—I had a feeling there was a bird in that hedgerow. The wind was coming due north into our faces, and I had no doubt she'd already smelled the occupants of the hedgerow, even at a hundred yards.

Once we got there, I gripped Maggie's collar firmly as Brian broke through the thick cover into the far field. Checking the wind once more, I found it still sympathetic to the plan. Brian would parallel me, but as much as thirty or forty yards in front, as I let Maggie loose in the hedgerow. If the bird did what it had done last time, it would run Maggie down the row and flush wild, hopefully in front of Brian. I would try to keep up with Maggie for as long as I could. The second I let her go, she was into the thorny hedgerow between Brian and me and moving at a maddening speed that was not humanly attainable.

It didn't take long.

As the rooster came out my side, I smiled—a bit too smugly—and drew down on him. He was forty yards out and moving away fast. Naturally, I missed him. That fact alone was bad enough. But just then two more roosters shot out wild on Brian, who had slowed down when he heard my shots. He tried a shot but was too far back and didn't draw any feathers.

"Three! Three wild birds!" I yelled to him.

When the fourth bird picked up *behind* us, I swung around fast enough to develop whiplash. Was it possible that this bird had allowed Maggie to chase the three others within inches of him but sat tight until we had passed by? I was willing to give the bird high marks for intelligence—until it flew around right in front of me. At ten yards I could see its bright eye staring at me in the rising sun. Letting the distance open up just a bit more, I placed my bead right on its beak and pulled the trigger at twenty yards.

And pulled. And pulled.

"Shoot it! Shoot it!" Brian was yelling through the screen of brush.

By the time I noticed the red shell poking out of the action at an odd angle, the bird was long gone.

"What are you doing?" Brian asked, coming through the hedge.

"It jammed."

"Four birds! There were four *roosters!*"

"I was there. I know."

Angrily shucking the jammed shell out of the action, I watched sadly as Maggie raced across the field after the last cockbird, chasing it a hundred yards to the far hedgerow. I thought I heard the bird flush out the far side, but it was hard to tell at that distance. A few moments later she appeared at the edge of the field once again and trotted back toward us, looking ruffled and depressed.

I couldn't blame her.

Back at the house, Greta asked, "So what did you get?"

"Did you hear all the shooting?" Brian asked.

"No."

"Good."

I decided to rest Ted at least another day before letting him out again, having no desire to suffer the wrath of my vet if his eye began clouding over again. Besides, it was exceptionally bright out this morning, and Ted's pupil was still somewhat dilated even though he had been off the medicine for a few days. That was a perfectly normal reaction, the vet told us over the phone. Before we left, I figured that my gun had been fouled up after an afternoon of excessive sporting clays shooting the previous weekend, causing the jam. The gas ports were probably fouled, but this sudden realization was lost in the preparations of getting Maggie food and water and loading the truck with all of our stuff. Had I stayed with this line of thought and either cleaned my shotgun or switched it for another before I left, I would have been saved more aggravation later in the day.

But I forgot all about it.

Walking up the trail by the lake, we listened to the tinkling of Maggie's metal tags as she merrily bounded through nasty thorns. Normally we would have fanned out a bit, but the brush was almost impenetrable, so we walked single file, with Greta in the lead. I really wanted her to get her first pheasant. She'd taken her first woodcock and her first rabbit this year. A ringneck would be the icing on the cake. Only a few moments passed before Maggie began crashing into instead of gingerly stepping through the thorns.

"She's birdy."

We stopped in the trail and listened to Maggie unravel the scent trail in the vicious thorns. Greta held her gun ready across her chest. I almost pitied the bird. It came up quickly, from right to her left front. She swung and missed with the first shot, and there were nearly simultaneous clicks as Brian and I took our safeties off. The second shot from Greta's autoloader sent a puff of feathers into the air as the bird dropped.

Greta turned around with something of a glare.

"Jeez, you guys! Do you know what it's like to hear those little clicks and see those guns going up out of the corner of your eye as you're trying to shoot?"

We were somewhat aware of the phenomenon but said nothing.

Maggie brought the bird out of the thorns and deposited it at our feet. Greta's nervousness with her hunting partners seemed to dissipate with the sight of the dog bringing in her first pheasant.

"Good girl, Maggie-May!"

We pocketed the big bird and continued on up the trail. Fifteen minutes later, another bird came up, this time from left to right, and I shot behind it twice. There was no third shot since my gun was once again jammed. Greta and Brian moaned in frustration behind me. Neither could get a safe shot with me in the lead.

"That's it. You guys take turns on point. I'll use the one-shot wondergun for backup."

Angry isn't the word.

After a lengthy drink from the creek far below us, Maggie finally decided to return—at her own pace— and before I could yell at her for ignoring the whistle, she promptly flushed another rooster. It towered above the treetops thirty yards to our right, silhouetted against the glowing orange of the creekbank oaks. We all had a clear shot at the bird, and I think everyone expected everyone else to shoot. Finally, with the bird apparently about to get off scot-free, *everyone* opened up. Even my gun fired twice, not jamming until the third shell. About that, I was something short of ecstatic.

The bird, for all the luck of its near escape, did not fare well in the final outcome. At least one of the five shots we threw tumbled it in midair. Far beyond a dense wall of thorns, the bird managed to right itself and lock wings, at least for a moment. Then it appeared to crash into the brush below. From our high vantage point, even Maggie could see where it went. She was gone like a shot while we tried picking a route down through the tugging mess of berries and briars. In some places the thorns were ten feet high, and I could do nothing more than put my rear to the brush and walk backward, trying to ignore the thorns that found their way in around the nylon face of my brush pants. Brian was right behind me; Greta seemed to be picking a clearer (and somewhat smarter) route down to the creek.

Suddenly, a desperate wailing filled our ears. *Maggie.* I didn't hear any wings beating. All I could picture was another raccoon, this one tearing the hell out of her with no shotgun to back her up.

"Joel! Get her!" Greta yelled.

As if I needed any more encouragement, I turned and ran headlong down through the evil thorns. I could hear Brian right behind me. We reached the high bank above the creek, but the sound had carried oddly on the steep banks and Maggie was eighty yards to our north, yowling and whining even more pathetically.

"Help her!" Greta said from far behind us.

You want me to go where?

I ran up the deer trail along the bank, slipping and nearly falling in the slick oak leaves. I checked the action of my gun, making sure a live round was in there for whatever had Maggie. This would be no time for a jammed shell. Rounding a small deadfall, we came face to face with my fearless dog. I looked around for the raccoon or possum or skunk (or lion or tiger or bear) but found nothing. Maggie wagged her tail at me, her eyes bright. Placing two paws on a young oak, she let go with another yip, this one less scary.

Twelve feet up in the crotch of the tree was our pheasant.

Brian and I began laughing. He used a long stick to dislodge the bird, and Maggie promptly pounced on it. When Greta caught up with us, she had that incredulous look again. Her hat was gone and she sported a nice scratch across her cheek—your typical pheasant-hunting scar. I didn't laugh, of course.

"Because of the bird?"

"She could see it up there. It was driving her crazy."

"*Jeez*," she said again, her fingers touching the red line on her cheek.

"Welcome to my world," I said, winking.

Back at the lake, we decided to try the brushy lots on the north side of the road. We'd never done very well there, but I knew it bordered a heavily posted, protected area where wild birds were staging something of a comeback. I had seen the birds in here several times over the past few winters while rabbit hunting with the dogs. I thought few others knew of this wild-bird population until I heard three guys at the sporting goods store up the road from my house remarking on the very same thing.

Oh, well.

Pulling into the small parking area overlooking some old boat docks on a murky Lake Ontario tributary, we climbed out of the truck with the field weariness of jaded bird hunters. We'd barely gotten the guns loaded and the vests zipped when the undeniable presence and relative density of the local ringneck population made themselves known. As we proceeded in single file up the trail through the dense, nasty undergrowth, Brian and Greta ahead of me signaled wildly at a rooster gliding from the posted preserve on our left to the dense undergrowth of the open hunting area to our right.

I heeled Maggie, who miraculously had not seen the flying bird. When we reached the spot where the pheasant must have landed, we broke into a drive line and turned right into the brush. Everyone's gun was held in that white-knuckled grip that only the knowledge of an impending flush can bring.

Brian moved into deep grass to the left. Greta, closer to me, flanked the edge of some thornapple trees where I thought the bird must have landed, if only out of spite for us. I crouched and entered the thornapple. Most of these trees, of the kind I have been stabbed by many times, are stand-alones or in clusters of as many as a half-dozen small ones. But this tangle was a veritable thornapple *forest*. Each time I rose above a deep crouch, I received a warning prick to the back of my neck or top of my head. Past experiences with the painful aftereffects stifled my desire to suffer another full-blown impaling.

I'm currently reading *Death in the Long Grass*, my second Peter Capstick book on the travails of pursuing dangerous game in Africa. I imagined this thorny tangle to be much like the ones he describes in which many a bold hunter met his untimely end at the claws, horns, teeth, or tusks of some savage beast. *Yes, this must be what it was like,* I thought, *the silence of the bush and the hunter's nerves are suddenly shattered by the thunder of a Cape buff.* Just then a bunny hopped by, with Maggie in nub-wagging pursuit. So much for my fantasy. I didn't shoot, even though there was a twenty-yard safety window between the dog and the cottontail. I knew that in this thick cover the concussion of the shot might cause the rooster to flush wild. He had to be in here somewhere, and the bird would be a far better prize than another plate of *hasenpfeffer.*

When Maggie came back from pursuing Peter Cottontail and my Capstick fantasy had been sufficiently ruined, we exited the thorny cover. We circled the general area once more but never did catch sight or scent of that bird. I wish I had a dollar for every time that has happened to me in the past few years. No, scratch that. I wish I had a *pheasant* for every time that has happened.

Continuing on up the narrow trail, we finally broke out into the long grass of a big field that overlooked the lake. Though the grass cover was immense, the entire area was dotted with acre and two-acre stands of dense saplings, from which we might well scare up a woodcock or two. It would also offer, I knew through experience, several handy escape routes for any birds we might get up and running. (I sincerely hoped for *up* rather than *running.*)

After working the first wide expanse of grass with no interest from Maggie, we stood at the edge of the first sapling island, foolishly trying to make a plan. Maggie milled around in the next grassy patch, a little too far ahead of us as we stood talking in the same driveline formation. Suddenly, Greta was peering hard into the grass at her right.

"It's a . . . Can you. . . ?"

"What?" I asked. "What do you see?"

"Can you shoot one on the ground?"

I was incredulous. I wanted to say, "No, it's not sporting," but somehow that never escaped my lips. Before the discussion of shooting ethics could continue, Greta disappeared, half-trotting, into the thick saplings, leaving Brian and me standing in the open, not saying a word. After another moment's worth of indecision, I finally called Maggie back and sent her in after Greta.

Not much time passed before the rooster flushed out of range, giving us all a glimpse of long tail

Greta's first pheasant.

feathers and a broad white neckband as he turned on the afterburners and disappeared. Figuring he was long gone, Brian and I were surprised to see him drop back down near the far edge of the thicket. We yelled to Greta, asking why she didn't shoot. The answer had something to do with being tangled in prickers and unable to see three feet in any direction, not to mention the utter impossibility of lifting her shotgun in the heavy brush, *thank you very much.* I didn't press the issue. Instead I left Greta stranded in the mess as Brian and I hurried around to the other side of the thicket.

Unbelievably, the rooster began cackling from somewhere near the base of a big cottonwood tree, the largest landmark in the sea of scrubby little saplings. Brian and I split up, trying to position ourselves to cover as much air as possible when my wife or the dog or both finally spooked the bird out. For a few moments, there was a symphony of sound from that round patch of cover surrounded on all sides by long grass. I could hear Maggie's tags jingling. I could hear sticks snapping and Greta muttering—she was getting a true bird hunter's initiation. More jingling. More snapping. And above it all, the rooster continued to cackle. At first I thought it might just be an agitation kind of thing, the bird letting the intruders know that *he* knew they were there and they were most unwelcome. But now, looking at it through the clarity of time, I suspect he was just taunting us, knowing he was safe in his little castle surrounded by a moat of nearly impenetrable brush.

Eventually, the bird quieted down, and Maggie exited the thicket with her tongue hanging down like a pendulum. Greta, however, remained entrenched.

"Come on out," I offered.

"That's fine. But which way might that *be?*"

"We'll go around, and you go back the way you came. We'll meet you back there."

Maggie moved lethargically ahead of us, tired from the morning's hunt and sluggish from the afternoon's heat. Our first order of business would be to head back to the creek for a drink. Just then, as so often happens, *everything* happened. Maggie picked up scent and disappeared around the outside of the thicket at a full run. Brian and I, too, kicked into some version of high gear, trotting around the corner.

"It makes sense," I said. "He slipped out the back door while nobody was watching."

"We've seen that before," Brian offered.

Reaching a small patch of golden grass on a large knoll, we were treated to the sight of Maggie dashing madly back and forth. Brian and I all but mounted our guns. We'd seen this before, too. I would eat my sweaty old hunting hat if Maggie didn't flush a bird. She was in overdrive. So was my heart.

When the hen flushed ten yards away, I'm sure it had no idea how close it came to being vaporized as Brian and I both snapped our shotguns up and slid off the safeties at precisely the same second. If the bird *had* realized this, it may well have died of fright. As it was, it flew away unscathed, much to the unbridled displeasure of Maggie, who glared back at me after giving the brown bird a short chase across the field.

"Roosters," I said *"Roosters."*

We finally found Greta, who was mumbling something about a short, fat bird running out ahead of her on the way out—the sun may have been getting to her, too.

We never did find that bird, but on the way out I was sure I heard him cackle again.

November's Doorstep

Not far from where we had, *um*, *treed* the bird a couple of days earlier, Brian and I pushed down through the same tangle of thorns and grappling-hook bushes on our way to the steep creek bank. What were we doing here again? Chasing another errant bird? No. Following Maggie, hot on scent? No, although my little springer was somewhere in the mess ahead of us. Had we lost our sanity?

Perhaps.

It's not as if we hadn't tried the easier, more open areas near the lake. Actually, we had hunted them fairly hard. Unlike a week earlier, when we'd limited, we simply hadn't seen any birds in the easy areas today. Not a trio prone to taking the easy way—when it comes to hunting, anyway—Brian and Mag and I let out a collective sigh, braced ourselves for puncture wounds, and headed into the disagreeable brush. Thorns tugged hungrily at us as we crackled and snapped and popped (not to mention tripped and cursed and swore) our way into the heavy thicket. But several scratches and colorful rephrasings of old familiar terms later, we were at the creek without even a rabbit flush to show for it. Sweating profusely, we looked over the edge and watched Maggie, already swimming far below us. From that elevation, we could see her legs pumping up and down as she, well, dog-paddled. At water's edge she shook herself dry and took a moment to inspect a tattered duck blind. Then she suddenly raced up the steep shale hill, probably thinking she'd sneaked off on us for her swim and now needed to hurry and catch back up. Only yards short of the top, she spotted us and lowered her head in a guilty dog-smile.

Figuring on trying the north side of the road, where the wild rooster had led Greta astray yesterday, we drove the short stretch to the other parking area, but disappointment met us in the shape of two men and two dogs preparing to go into the cover. We stopped for a drink before driving south through the little town of Wilson, where I went to high school and learned the art of flyfishing for steelhead at the tender age of thirteen (a much better education than the one I received within the dull red brick walls of Wilson Central High). The town hadn't changed much since the days of my forgotten homework assignments and failed algebra tests. Large shade trees still overhung the nicely middle-class houses on Main Street. Beyond the houses, there were no blocks of development like there are in so many other corners of the county. Between Wilson and Cambria are just a sprinkling of houses and a few dozen farms that have not *yet* (and I stress that word with a sad sigh) sold their road frontage off in small, erosive chunks to land developers.

There were still pheasants here. You couldn't prove it by our morning's lack of success, but the birds were around, and I pray that by the time you read this, they will still be there.

At the same corner of two back roads where we'd been disappointed to find a pair of hunters last week, we found the long grass dried by the late morning sun and the large field thankfully empty of orange hats and tan vests. Maggie, showing some strain now, hesitated about jumping off the tailgate. In return, I hesitated to lift her down, fearing she might need a well-deserved rest. Ted was back on the roster now, but doing only half-duty as an injured reserve. I carefully lifted Maggie down and set her in the grass by the road. How much weight she'd shed in the past weeks was not lost on me. But once her paws touched the grass, it was as if someone had lit a firecracker near her wagging nub. She was hunting before we were loaded.

Good old Mag.

On the west end of the long field are several stands of high, cattail-like weeds reaching ten or twelve feet in the air. Their interior is a mini bamboo jungle, and wherever we find these patches, we find critters. There is something about the deep recesses of the thick shoots that attracts game animals. The only other great patch of these weeds we regularly hunted was on the eighty-two acres we lost. *(Stop whining about it already, Spring. They are gone!)* There was a patch near the road that never failed to produce a bird or rabbit. It was the magician's hat of our hunts, and we always managed to pull something out of it. Even before the entire eighty-two acres sold (I'm almost done with it now, so be patient), two little parcels were sold off to a developer. The first thing they did was to put bright orange surveyor's tape around a previously indefinable patch of dogwoods with a patch of high weeds right in the center. You guessed it: In the center of those innocuous-looking little red flags, a house sprang up—and an ugly one to boot. I can't drive by that house (I avoid doing so if at all possible) and not think about the wonderful piece of upland cover once located approximately where the tacky new dining room must be. Now there isn't a sprig of dogwood within a hundred yards of the place; instead, some bulldozed semi-flat sections were festooned with cheap grass seed in what I assume the owner deems his "lawn."

Where was I? Oh, yes, pheasant hunting. So while Maggie crashed around in the tall mini-jungle, Brian and I flanked the piece of cover, often taking a tentative step this way and that, trying to catch a glimpse of brown and white or, if we were incredibly lucky, the sight of a rooster pheasant trying to outmaneuver my dog on foot.

For a moment the familiar sounds of sniffing and jingling dog tags stopped. The sudden vacuum of sound ended with beating wings as a pheasant took off directly into the sun. Once it turned, revealing the plain tan and brown plumage of a hen, we reluctantly lowered our guns.

Heading home, late season.

'I'his was the one and only place I'd mistakenly shot a hen pheasant. It had happened early on in my bird-hunting career. She'd taken off from an identical patch of weeds not fifty yards from where we now stood. She'd gone into the sun as well. Once the dog had fetched her to me, I thought I had lost my mind—I would have *sworn* she cackled like a fine old rooster when she came up. The silhouette she offered against the morning sun was one of long tail feathers and a plump body. There was no doubt in my mind that I was shooting a rooster. Of course, in the end, I was wrong.

We'd followed Maggie about a quarter of the length of the tediously long, straight field when she accelerated into a run. She had appeared to be slowing from the abnormal warmth of the day, and I was starting to feel sorry for her. But suddenly her nose had filled with scent, triggering in her lithe forty-pound frame another of the energy reserves of which she seems to have an endless supply. She was off, and it was all we could do to catch up. Last year a rooster had run from this very same spot, escaping out the end of the field and into the huge sea of corn beyond. I thought it not absurd that this might be that same bird. In a hasty plan that reeked of, well, hasty planning, I decided I would let Brian chase Maggie while I raced out ahead of them and down to the end of the field to cut the bird off. It sounded good on paper. As it turned out, I ended up about sixty yards behind Maggie when she vanished through the hedgerow, presumably flushing the bird wild out the other side. I presumed this because Maggie came back to me in short order, begging for a drink. The length of her tongue (approximately two feet) and the rapidity of its lolling (twenty-five pants per second) made me very glad I'd brought her little plastic water bottle. She greedily slurped it from my hand while lying down. Brian came up behind us, his hat in his hand, sweating as badly as I. The three of us sat in the grass and rested for a few moments. We didn't need to say a word. It had to have been a rooster. Maybe *the* rooster.

Watching Maggie rise after her four-minute rejuvenation period, I noticed that her front-leg gimpiness was back. *That's it,* I thought. We headed for the truck by way of a thick hedgerow. Maggie trotted along slowly right between Brian and me. If anything was nearby, she might have picked up its scent, but she was not actively hunting. Brian was saying something to me when Maggie froze with one paw lifted in the air, showing a bit of her muddled ancestry that contains a pointer or two. Abruptly, she was off on a tear—in the opposite direction.

I ran as far as I could, my feet bogging down in the clinging black dirt of the cornfield's edge, while Brian raced along in the grass of the big field. Since I hadn't heard her collar jingling for several seconds, I knew Maggie was bound to flush another one wild.

These birds can be tough.

"Had to be another bird," I said.

On cue, the rabbit burst from the hedgerow and paused at the edge of the corn. I waited for it to head away, but it ran right at me, probably because of the sound of the approaching dog. At thirty yards, sure that Maggie was safe in the hedgerow and nowhere behind the target, I touched the trigger.

Maggie erupted from the hedgerow fifty yards farther down and lowered her head, sniffing furiously and automatically switching to after-the-shot fetch mode. When she found the rabbit, she didn't pounce on it with glee, but dutifully carried it to me and dropped it at my feet. When she'd spat out an adequate amount of bunny fur, occasionally gagging, she headed directly for the truck. I had to help her in. I just wish someone had been there to help *me* in. Although it was only noon, we were done, by any definition of the word.

I cooled my heels in late afternoon at one of my bow stands out behind the house. I could have just gone home and crashed on the couch—probably *should* have—but vacation time is scarce. Settling into my perch fourteen feet above the forest floor, I let the wind, from the northwest now and a bit cooler, chill my back. The relative quiet of the evening nearly lulled me to sleep. Not wanting to awaken hanging like a rag doll from my safety belt, I stood up and stretched.

The doe that had moved silently in behind me stomped her foot in the dry leaves, and I recognized the sound at once. Several moments passed before she allowed that I *might* be just a big fat raccoon stretching in that tree, and she led her fawn past me. Their acorn munching was clearly audible as they passed on the trail, vacuuming the forest floor for tidbits. A moment after they disappeared, a spike buck appeared and I lifted the bow off the hanger, though I had no real intention of killing him. I enjoyed that selfish, Godlike feeling of dominion as I let him pass, let him live.

Darkness came shortly after.

On the way out, several woodcock flitted before my eyes against the amber sky of the fallen sun. Here, on November's doorstep, I was brought back mentally to the night in September when I'd set out on my ATV near dark and watched the birds fly in. Now, a couple of months later and into the heart of bird season, I was more tired than I had been that night and was less filled with anticipation. Things tonight were different, but not in a bad way. Standing rock-still, I watched another pair of woodcock dive into a small opening in the slash ahead of me. Back in the truer darkness of the woods, an owl hooted as I smiled, happy with my life.

Who Needs Rest?

John and Steve both called, eager to get out this afternoon, but Maggie still looked bad. With Ted's eye on the mend, I was not completely against taking him out on what promised to be a fine, cool Friday evening, but wasn't crazy about the idea. Hoping Maggie would make a miraculous recovery once out in the fresh air, I took her out in late morning for a practice run up the ditch across the road. I almost didn't take my gun, but knowing that was a clear and willful violation of my own rules, I pinned my hunting license to my coat and loaded the .410 as I walked down the driveway.

At first, Maggie hobbled along behind me, and things weren't looking hopeful for her hunting prospects the next day or two. But as I had hoped, once she set foot into the bush-hogged grass and brush of the ditch, she picked up her pace a bit. And when she caught scent of something—probably a rabbit—she dashed into the shade of some pines at the edge of the ditch. Tensing my hand around the tiny stock of the .410, I listened to Maggie snuffing and snorting in there, expecting a rabbit to zip out at any second. When she emerged, still badly favoring that right front leg, I gave it up and turned back for the house.

"You need a break, girl."

Her nub wagged, though I didn't sense any firm agreement on her part. With Greta at work and the kids at school, the house was empty (except for me, the two dogs, the two cats, a goldfish tank, and an aquarium full of pregnant mollies). I figured I'd take advantage of the peace and work on several things that needed attending to around here. There were leaves to rake, letters and proposals to write. Naturally, I stretched out on the couch and fell asleep. I didn't realize how badly I needed it until I woke up three hours later. Maggie was watching with her paws up on the picture window as Greta pulled into the driveway, home from work. Ted was curled in a tight, black ball on the opposite end of the couch, snoring soundly.

"Hey, you better get down quick!"

He did, and was stretching innocently as Greta walked through the door.

An hour later, I had to meet John and Steve and was coming to the stiff realization that I could easily have spent another ten or twelve hours on the couch. According to Greta, I looked in worse shape than the dogs. And neither one of them was going to win any poise contests. For the first time in a long while, I was beginning to get whupped.

Ahhhhh, pheasant season.

With a close eye on the clock, I gathered up my vest and gun and whistle and leash and filled the water bucket. Ted followed me around the house, shadowing my every move. He'd been left home so many times that he wasn't acting extremely excited, as is his norm, but was watching me closely. Both dogs knew well the obvious preparations for a bird hunt. When I stepped out of my jeans and into my brush pants, two large black paws nearly took me off my feet.

"You want to get birds today?"

He was gone and waiting by the back door before I had my second leg in the brush pants. To my amazement, Maggie was nowhere to be seen. She never failed to get excited when she saw the hunting preparations being made. Walking around the house, I searched for my bird dog and finally found her curled up behind the blue chair in the living room with her eyes squinted shut, giving the appearance of a child who hopes fervently that if she doesn't open her eyes, you won't be able to see her, either. I hadn't seen Maggie avoid the chance to go hunting before, or since. I guess that illustrates how tired she was. I knew the feeling.

Ted, at least, was excited.

Author and Ted with a ringneck limit.

Follow that tail!

John and Minnie were waiting in the parking area near the lake. While we waited for Steve, Minnie and Ted passed the time by thoroughly sniffing each other and doing the other things dogs—particularly Labs—do in each other's company. As Steve's red Jeep came up the road, I loaded my gun and quickly snapped the leash on Ted, who was just a little *too* eager to be in the brush and hunting. Steve hadn't ever killed a pheasant, and I didn't want a rooster flushing from the brush near the road as he pulled up. Still groggy from the aftereffects of my three-hour departure from consciousness, I listened to John and Steve talk excitedly about the afternoon's prospects. I remembered being like that a long time ago—or maybe just yesterday. I forget. Once everyone was geared and loaded up, we headed out on the same narrow trail that Greta and Brian and I had ended up on the other day. I cradled my side-by with one hand and stifled a yawn with the other.

"Wake up!" said some much more cheery and enthusiastic hunter.

I yawned again. John and I walked shoulder to shoulder with Steve behind us as the dogs disappeared up the trail. I couldn't help yawning widely and loudly once more.

"Would you stop that, already?" John said, laughing.

A split-second later, I quickly woke up as three rooster pheasants rocketed from the cover not twenty yards from us. The birds split in three directions, and, naturally, John and I picked the same bird to shoot at as the two others escaped over the top of the dogwoods.

Unsheathing my camera, I trotted up a side trail to where Ted was already fetching the bird out of the brush and took some close-ups of him coming toward me. I mean *closeups:* I actually had to wipe feathers off the camera lens after he'd pushed the bird right into it.

I wasn't tired anymore. The yawns were gone. Two more birds were out there in the brush, and we were going to get them! What luck to locate them this near the road, and neither one appeared to fly more than sixty or seventy yards. We had to take a break as John threw the dead pheasant for Minnie, trying to give her some "real" retriever practice since he hadn't had much time to hunt with her this year. I was anxious to get on the other birds but understood the process. We'd done the same thing with Maggie and Ted, and they turned into fine retrievers. Of course, Ted wanted nothing to do with letting Minnie retrieve *his* pheasant (dogs are funny that way) and did his best to disrupt the fetching drills, most commonly by pouncing on the puppy and yanking the bird out of her mouth. Ted is many things, but subtle is nowhere on the list. Rather than leash him and curb his enthusiasm, Steve and I continued with him on up the trail while John threw the bird a few more times for Minnie.

A few dozen yards later, with John back in the fold, one of the single roosters went up to the right. Steve was on the bird, his gun snapping smartly up, when for reasons I still don't fully understand, even months later, John yelled, *"Hen! Don't shoot!"*

The muzzle of Steve's shotgun wavered, and I tried forcing out the words caught in my throat like a gallon of bad mouthwash. They finally came out: *"Take it!!!"*

Steve thankfully didn't hesitate, and his first rooster pheasant folded at thirty yards with that satisfying *poof* of feathers known to pheasant hunters the world around.

"Yes!"

Somewhere among the backslapping and Ted's trotting the final few yards to retrieve the bird, the third ringneck went up squarely in front of John and heading from right to left in a big hurry. That bird went off like a mortar shell, taking us by surprise. John, the only one with a shot, raised his autoloader and *bang-bang-banged*, but the bird continued on down the field. Ted raced off like a greyhound, his eyes locked on the bird. John raced after him. Steve and I stood there, astounded at the amount of action in the tiny slice of time. Finally, I went and retrieved Steve's bird myself, since Ted seemed to be otherwise occupied.

"Good boy!" Steve said.

"Woof."

A moment later I heard John yelling for Ted and Minnie and then *bang-bang*. We listened for his call to "Fetch it up," but it never came. Hurrying down the field, Steve

Steve Olsen with his first rooster pheasant.

and I found John staring at a wall of dogwood. We could hear the dogs working in there, not far from the edge.

"Did you get him?" Steve asked.

"He didn't go . . . I mean, he's in here. I might have missed him."

I started laughing, but John didn't think it was all that funny. A few moments later, when we were all deep in the thick, slapping cover watching the dogs look fruitlessly for scent where John thought the bird had gone down, I didn't think it was all that funny, either. We circled and scoured and backtracked and front-tracked. The dogs weren't scenting anything, dead or alive.

"He *has* to be in here," John insisted.

Yeah, right.

We spent another hour, until the sun began nearing the treetops, looking for places where the bird might have shot out into the open field, running for its life, but the dogs never picked up anything. But we had two birds, and it was hard to complain about that. Of course, John still complained.

An hour before dark, we went to the field where the wild rooster (or whatever it was) had run Brian and Maggie and me downfield shortly before I shot the rabbit. Another guy was there, barely visible in his brown coat and tan cap even in the yellow rays of the brilliant late-afternoon sun. Since he appeared to be heading out, we waited until he got near the road and headed in. I didn't spot a dog anywhere near him.

Ted and Minnie, who's learning a bit about fetching.

"How'd you do?" I asked.

He smiled, "Nice rooster in the back corner."

No. Not without a dog! Couldn't be. Simply *impossible.*

"Hey, that's great." I said.

Just then, a small female Brittany materialized, seemingly from the grass itself, and trotted up to us for a sniff.

Whew.

Once the other hunter was gone, we plowed headlong into the field and started making time, keeping the setting sun at our back. I had no desire for any more rooster/hen mixups today. If something flushed into that brilliant orange globe, it would be impossible to tell if it was a pheasant or a hawk, much less a hen or a rooster. I was feeling a bit glum, thinking that the guy who just left might have killed that same wily rooster that had evaded us for the past couple of years.

Nah.

Near the middle of the field, Ted began getting crazy—and I don't use the term lightly—bouncing from left to right as if slamming into unseen Plexiglas walls. His movements were so herky-jerky that it looked like he was having a seizure. I began racing toward him, yelling to encourage John and Steve to do the same. When the hen lifted off, its plumage caught the sunlight and the bird seemed to hang there, beautiful in a plain way, above the golden grass before departing for coverts unknown.

When Ted looked back at us for further direction, his healing eye caught the sun in an eerie glow. Feeling for the camera, I was disappointed to find I'd left it in the truck after our lakeside hunt.

On the way back to the vehicles, Ted and Minnie still sniffed here and there but showed obvious signs of their tiredness. It had been a long day, but I wasn't complaining. I was just glad I hadn't opted for another nap.

Saturday at the Club

Though wild-bird season was still open and I *swore* I was going to hunt only wild birds, I wanted to keep in contact with the new friends I was making at the club. It wasn't as if we weren't getting any birds—sure, it had taken until that first Thursday to get warmed up, but we'd bagged a few. However, I felt like treating myself to a day of hunting birds that didn't necessarily have the IQ of a Ph.D.

Maggie was stiff when the alarm went off at 6 A.M., but as she watched my progression from the coffeepot to the hallway, from my bathrobe to my brush pants, she ran excitedly up and down the length of our small house. Hitting one end of the hallway, she'd skid to a stop and race back the other way. Her stiffness melted away, possibly fanned out of her by way of her frantically wagging nub. As I sat at the table and drank my coffee, bleary-eyed, she would put her paws on my legs and push off of me, whining quietly and yawning too much. She wouldn't even eat breakfast.

She was ready.

There wasn't much of a turnout for a perfect, sunny, 40-degree morning. Not that I was complaining, of course. The few attendees were the regulars, though a couple of the closer friends I'd made didn't show up. Everyone was paired up when the last bit of coffee was drunk and the sun had sufficiently risen. Boots clunked and paws scrambled across the clubhouse floor as we headed for the fields.

As an afterthought, one of the guys out hunting with his cousin asked me to join up with them. As nice as the offer was, I thought it would be even nicer to enjoy a couple hours alone trailing behind Maggie. Things were never boring hunting with Mag, and I knew I wouldn't be wishing for more company. The line of men dispersed across the open fields behind the clubhouse. Five of them headed for the back field, which surprised me. I usually had that one to myself.

No matter. I was in an exceptionally good mood and had a number of other places to hunt. The pair of guys to my left began cutting slightly in front of me, and I hung back. I knew one of the guys, but the other was his guest. I granted them the right-of-way, waving them on when they looked back and realized they'd angled into my path. With Maggie still on the leash, I watched the two men and their shorthair disappear into the brush near the back of the skeet fields. Maggie whined softly.

"Patience," I said, as if I had any of my own. I was feeling rather peaceful and didn't mind waiting a few minutes before I had to breathlessly chase Maggie all over creation. *Just let the coffee settle in. Let the other hunters establish their routes. No rush.* Oh, yeah, I was Mr. Cool. The silence of the chilly morning air and the peace of my early morning thoughts were both disrupted by a shot, and another, then another. By the sounds, they'd come from the far field. *My* field. Shortly after the volley, I heard the fetch whistle, quickly followed by another volley, again from that far field. Maggie tugged at the leash, looking through the woods in the direction of the shots.

"Easy, girl, that's just people stealing *our* birds," said Mr. Cool, who wasn't the least bit jealous.

I could still hear the jingle of the bell (damned annoying, that practice) on the collar of the shorthair in the brush far ahead of us. My plan was to wait until they were safely on their way, then cut across their backtrail and angle out away from their route.

My hand was on the snap ring of Maggie's leash when I heard the cackle of a flushing rooster and the pair in front of me opened up. Birdshot from the trio of blasts snickered into the brush twenty yards ahead of me. The rooster appeared a moment later, locking his wings in full view, sixty yards ahead of Maggie and me. Flaring up—at the sight of us in the field, I imagine—he set his wings and dropped hard into the edge of some saplings, precisely in the tiny opening where the two hunters had entered the brush.

Maggie, who had watched the bird's landing, was a basket case. Straining at the leash, she choked herself, coughing and gagging. Whining and occasionally barking, her misery was apparent.

"Easy, girl. We can't just steal it. I mean . . . we have to wait a little at least, right?"

She did not agree, continuing to test the resiliency of the nylon leash, not to mention the aching forearm to which it was firmly attached.

After a few minutes passed and the voices and bells of the men and their dog finally vanished in the distance, I walked Maggie—fruitlessly trying to heel her—to within thirty yards of the brush. Had I been foolish enough to let her go any sooner, I knew I would be watching that rooster fly right back where it had come from. Unsnapping the leash that I estimate was being strained by a pressure of approximately twenty tons per square inch, I felt it slap back into my legs, and Maggie was off. I coiled the leash around my hand and tried to stuff it in the pocket of the vest—*quickly.*

Maggie was birdy already. She'd pinpointed the exact bush at which the bird landed—I know because I, too, had marked it—and covered the thirty or so yards to it in less time than it took me to straighten up after bending over to unhook her. Though expecting some trickery by the bird—I was getting used to chasing wild pheasants again—I was not ready when it went up. It didn't cackle, but towered above the treetops—an easy shot if I'd had my gun up. Shaking my hand free of the leash and the vest pocket, I mounted the shotgun and fired. The first shot went, I knew instantly, well behind the bird, which was now accelerating out toward the open field. *If I blow this one,* I thought, *Maggie may leave me for another hunter.* Thankfully the bird crumpled at the second shot, and I didn't have to go shopping for a new springer puppy.

Maggie has the prettiest retrieve. I mean, sure, it's just a little springer carrying in a huge bird, not a rare occurrence on this planet, but the way she does it is something special. At no time during the hunting day does Maggie stop or even slow down unless forced to do so, but when she carries birds back to me—or rabbits, for that matter—she steps delicately, placing one foot carefully on the ground at a time, her prize held high enough so that even the tail feathers of the biggest rooster don't drag on the earth. She is just the picture of *pride.* It was no different this morning. Coming to me in slow motion, she cradled the big cockbird, perfectly balancing its fat body in her small jaws. At my side, she cocked her head and dropped the bird into my hand. Not even allowing a second for me to pat her on the head, Maggie shot back into the brush. No more slow motion.

Back to *fast-forward.*

I shadowed Maggie along one of the drainage ditches at the edge of the woods. She looked fine, showing no signs of the lameness she had been exhibiting on and off for the last couple of days. Working as always too far ahead of me, she didn't notice a rabbit that flushed across her back trail and nearly ran me over. I didn't shoot it, content that we would find some more birds. Anyway, it was too close, and I had no desire to clean one more rabbit taken with a heavy pheasant load at short range. There were plenty of those in the freezer already. Someday I may invent a meat-sifter to remove all those pellets. We followed the ditch to the end and were about to head west when a single shot rang out surprisingly close.

"Fetch it up!" a faint voice said.

I turned my back to the west and began walking. Maggie, sensing the direction change a few minutes late, raced past me so she could maneuver into her normal out-of-range position.

"Nice of you to join me."

Her nub wagged and I *swear* she winked at me on the way by.

Someone had had the presence of mind to cut four parallel paths through a dense dogwood thicket, and it was rapidly becoming my *second* favorite place to bird hunt. I'd shot more woodcock than pheasants on those trails, but that was OK, too. Working up one trail, we eventually came out to the big field and spotted two guys with a golden retriever. I hadn't seen them earlier at the clubhouse, although I'd met one of them before. Slightly disappointed at the amount of attention my field was getting, I turned back up one of the parallel rows and worked back through the dogwoods. Maggie pounced and sniffed and pranced through the cover, but, as with our first pass, we didn't flush a thing. Reaching the end where we'd started, we cut back on yet another trail, determined to cover the entire thicket. *If only the wild-bird coverts had trails like these,* I thought, *it would be so much easier. What are you saying, Spring?* (Perhaps I was becoming a bit schizophrenic.) *You could arm your shotgun with heat-seeking missiles, and hunting wild pheasants still wouldn't be easy.*

When we'd exhausted the final trail through the thicket, I sat down at the field's edge and called Maggie to me. Unfortunately, she got short-circuited by the ditch and lay down in it, taking long drinks and lounging in the chest-deep water. When she'd finally had her fill, she came over to me, and I began picking briars out of

Maggie, mugging with a longtailed rooster.

her silky coat. But I quickly gave up for now, knowing that essentially all I was doing was making some free space on her hide for the new ones she would undoubtedly pick up between now and quitting time. Snapping the leash on Maggie, I walked her slowly back through the brush and out toward the big field one more time. Maggie was tired enough that she didn't pull against the leash, heeling nicely along and bumping her nose into the game bag three or four times to make sure her rooster was still in there. I climbed up on a stump and scanned the gargantuan field for the sight of blaze-orange caps. Nobody.

Perfect.

I let Maggie go, and once again she was off like a shot. We went at nearly warp speed up one hedgerow, and I was certain that at any moment a bird was bound to flush. *Hens and roosters,* I kept telling myself, hens *and* roosters. Since wild-bird season had opened, I'd become re-accustomed to lowering my gun when a hen went up, and I had to remember that at the club either sex was fair game. Maggie sped up near where the hedgerow crossed into another perpendicular one. I was just positive a bird would go up. Suddenly, Maggie simply stopped and looked back at me and wagged her nub. I had been running full out, and I stopped, out of breath.

"What was that all about?"

Ignoring the question, Maggie went back to slowly probing the brush of the adjacent hedgerow. It took fifteen minutes to walk that one to completion and make another turn up yet another row that would take us around the third side of the large square we were outlining. Nearing the end of the third leg, Maggie began to slow down even more, briefly lying down in a puddle for a break and a tepid, brownish drink. I pulled the water bottle out of the vest (after prying it free from under the rooster), but by then she was done and didn't need any of *my* water, thank you very much. After skipping over twenty or thirty yards of the hedgerow, Maggie reentered it. I was about to hand-signal her to check out the part she'd missed when the bird went up. This one, too, took me by surprise.

It looked like a seagull, and I raised, then lowered, then raised the gun again. By the time I realized I was looking at a pure white pheasant, the bird was already in flight through a notch in the hedgerow, giving me a tail-end view and a shooting window approximately two feet wide. I filled that window with lead shot as fast as I could—three times.

The bird swung back around the far edge of the hedgerow, nearly a hundred yards away. Luckily, Maggie couldn't see it. The white bird was an impressive sight as it sailed off across the field and landed back in the thicket with the lovely bush-hogged trails through it. I immediately took off in that direction, keeping one eye on Maggie, who seemed reluctant to abandon the hedgerow just yet. I knew it would be wise to pay attention to her but at the same time hoped she was just sniffing around where the white one had flushed. A moment later Maggie was back alongside me. When she established the general direction I was heading, she took her place forty or fifty yards ahead. I readied myself for the flush, watching the ground cover carefully. *That bird should stand out like a sore thumb*, I thought. Turns out it was a well-hidden sore thumb.

It had appeared to land in some nasty briars near the upper end of an old bass pond, so I immediately signaled Maggie into the worst stuff. If the bird was there, she would root it out. But she didn't. In ever-widening circles, we orbited the thicket. Nothing. Finally we repeated the up-and-down-the-trail routine we'd done earlier, to see if Maggie could catch the bird's scent on the steady northeast breeze. She didn't. Not so much as a snort. I *knew* the bird was in there. I thought I'd seen it drop like a rock, but it must have continued on over the pond. So we tried the other side of the pond for the next twenty minutes. Nothing.

Though she was still hunting well, Maggie wasn't showing the least bit of interest in the general area where the bird had to be. Feeling the solid weight of the rooster in my vest and the burning in my

Author and Maggie with an odd white pheasant.

thighs that hadn't gone away for ten or twelve days straight now, I knew it was time.

"Let's go back to the truck."

Halfway up the big field, I was surprised to see a pickup truck parked partway up the lane. Two men sat on the tailgate combing out the large golden retriever with which I'd seen them hunting. After introductions—possibly reintroductions, since I am so bad at remembering names—the younger of the two spoke up.

"You didn't happen to see that white one, did you?"

"Oh . . . you saw my miss," I said, somewhat embarrassed. I thought the field had been empty.

"Oh, no," said the older of the two, the father. "We just saw her sitting in an apple tree on the way out just now. Over by the north end of the pond."

"Really? I'll be darned."

It made sense now. We *had* been in the right area. We just hadn't looked up. I'd been so intent on spotting that big white bird on the ground, I never thought about the trees.

"Yeah. She didn't even fly when we walked by . . . just kind of crouched down, making like she was invisible up there. We thought she was a snowy owl at first."

They both laughed.

When they were gone, I unsnapped Maggie's leash one last time that day and headed back the way we'd just come. Sure enough, there she was. We'd walked right under her, at least twice. Having no desire to shoot her out of the tree, I was surprised when she spooked at the sight of Maggie weaving around under her once again. Flushing straight up, the hen got her bearings and headed back across the field. My gun came up without hesitation this time. *Fool me once, shame on you,* I thought as I tucked the odd white pheasant into my game vest.

Now it was time to go home.

CHAPTER FIVE

THE FINAL ROUND

Me & Joe . . . & Steve . . . & Joe

Although I didn't know him very well yet, Joe already rated pretty high on my scale of decent human beings. (You can take that to mean that he was willing to hunt birds with me, one of the strictest criteria I have—in fact, one of the very few criteria I have, I am sad to say.)

With daybreak only a few moments past, we set out into one of the long fields near Pendleton with birdhunting on our minds. (Not that much else is on my mind in October or November or any other time, for that matter, but I digress—again.) Joe and I walked shoulder to shoulder up the trail between two long fields as Ted quartered back and forth in front of us, cutting from one field into the path and then into the next field, then back again. The trail was wide, so it seemed like a lot of wasted effort on Ted's part. It was time to get into the grass, time to start hunting.

I'd heard from other hunting acquaintances that Joe was an excellent trap and skeet shooter. I tried not to hold this against him since, although we were only fifteen minutes into our first hunt together, he seemed to be a genuine, pleasant person. That fact did not stop me from praying that if a bird came up, it would flush in front of him so I wouldn't be forced to display my own wingshooting prowess, which seems to get incrementally worse in direct proportion to how well my partners are able to shoot. Give me a bad shooter as a hunting partner and I will hit those birds every time. But give me a skeet champion and I'm destined to empty my gun at retreating birds (and usually the hail of lead is followed closely by a hail of four-letter words). So when Ted started getting birdy, my heart began pumping a bit faster than the excitement of the hunt dictated. *Please let it come up in front of Joe*, I thought. *Please.*

As quickly as he got excited, Ted slowed back down, and I figured he'd probably just picked up some old rabbit scent. Unlike Maggie, who will chase rabbits nearly as hard as pheasants, Ted can take them or leave them.

Ted with late-season hen pheasant.

"I haven't shot a bird in so long, I'm not sure I even remember how to do it," Joe said.

Yeah, right.

"Well, tell you what," I offered. "I'll hang back a bit if Ted gets birdy again, and you can take the shot." (I'm just nice that way.)

"No, we're hunting your dog. You shoot."

"No, I insist. *Really.* You take the shot, Joe. I have plenty of birds already. You're up."

"Well, thanks. I really appreciate that."

See how well things work out?

"So you've done pretty well this year?" he asked.

"I've gotten a few wild birds, a few state birds, and a few club birds. So, yeah, it's been a good one."

"I just can't tell you the last time I shot a pheasant," he began again. "It's been a. . . ."

From somewhere just off the end of Ted's nose, a large rooster rose out of some stubbly corn at the edge of the field. I stopped and watched the bird come up— over the barrel of my gun. Old habits die hard. The rooster, in a display of terminal stupidity, flew directly at Joe. This was one for instant replay: With the bird picking up speed, I willed Joe to shoot, but it didn't happen. As the bird got closer and closer, I lowered my own gun. At fifteen yards and gaining in altitude, the bird crumpled in an explosion of feathers as Joe fired the top barrel of his gun. The pheasant succumbed to the laws of gravity, and Joe succumbed to the laws of momentum as the bird smacked directly into his upper thighs. I started laughing as Ted raced in and picked it up. Ted handed Joe the bird, fulfilling his retrieving duties, however unnecessary they might have been under the circumstances.

"I guess you got your bird," I ventured.

"I guess so!"

Each blade of switchgrass has roughly ten billion microscopic teeth per square inch (I just made that up). The stuff tugs at your pants and tends to slow you down several miles per hour as you wade through a field of it. But it's great for birds. They get in and tunnel under it and can sit virtually undetectable from only a few feet, often sitting tight and letting you walk right by rather than flushing. Unfortunately, those serrated grass blades were serving another function today: They were meddling with Ted's tender eye. I didn't notice at first, since he was hunting so enthusiastically, but an hour or so into the field I noticed he was running with his head severely canted to one side to protect the sore eye. He was still hunting hard and it seemed a shame to quit, so I decided we'd head into the edge of the woods, where the grass still provided enough cover for ringnecks but wouldn't be so hard on Ted. I knew we would be more likely to flush woodcock or a rabbit there. Joe was agreeable, especially now that he was sporting several pounds of game bird in the back of his hunting vest.

I suspect we had been pushing a rooster along ahead of us in the grass, but I could be wrong. Either way, we had just exited the grasp of the switchgrass and eased into the brushy edge of the woodlot when another pheasant went up. It was a long flush, a shot I probably wouldn't have taken, but Joe shot and shot again. The rooster rose over a row of pine trees and disappeared back into the field from where we had just come.

"I probably shouldn't have shot," Joe said, shaking his head and reloading.

"Oh . . . he was shootable."

I know, I know, I am shameless.

Deeper into the shade of the woods, Ted worked tighter and tighter circles around the base of a tall white oak. Although there was nothing but bare ground below the tree, he just would not leave it alone.

"Come on, Teddy, it's just a squirrel."

On cue, the woodcock flushed, peeping wildly and flying at my face like a rabid bat. I swung around with the bird and began shooting as soon as he cleared my hat. The nice thing about an autoloader is that you can embarrass yourself not once or twice, as you can with a double barrel, but as many times as you are foolish enough to shoot. Four, in my case.

Joe's eyes were wide with a smile when I turned around. "Shootable, Joel?"

Hah, hah.

Two more woodcock went up before I finally hit one. Joe didn't shoot at any of the four birds. He was twenty years older than I, and I can only guess that his hesitation was an exhibition of the wisdom that comes with age.

I was supposed to meet my brother-in-law and nephew at 10:30 and, looking at my watch, knew I'd better go if I wanted to have time to swing home and trade off Ted for Maggie. As we quickly hunted our way out of the field, it was terribly difficult to ignore the rooster cackling mercilessly from the center of the switchgrass. *I'll be back,* I thought in true Terminator style complete with the bad Austrian accent.

On the way to Wilson, I called John on the cell phone and invited him to come along. I wasn't surprised when he accepted—pheasant season is only so long.

We were soon back. Only several yards up the trail again, Maggie flushed a large rooster. It happened so fast and in such concentrated cover that nobody got off a shot. I hung back with Eric while John and Steve took the lead behind Maggie. My legs were already burning from the morning's hike, and I was acting more in the capacity of a guide than a hunter. We worked the lake side of the road for an hour or more, directing Maggie in the general direction we believed the bird had gone, but she never put it up again. It could have flown all the way across the lake to Toronto for the amount of scent she picked up.

A rabbit zoomed right over the top of my boot and disappeared into a hole. Maggie was just behind it and slammed into me. Shaking herself off, she stuck her head into the hole and woofed once before looking at me and smiling.

"Birds, Maggie. *Birds*."

With a look of agonized panic, Steve suddenly said, "Oh, no . . . I lost my back-tag."

All four of us simultaneously turned around and looked back into the disagreeable tangle of brush from which we had just emerged. It wouldn't be impossible to backtrack, but nearly so. John and Steve went back in. I skirted the thicket with Eric under the guise of going back to the truck to get Maggie a drink since she looked overheated. Panting heavily, Maggie played the role perfectly. After she drank heartily from her green Coleman cooler (she really *was* thirsty), we headed back in and found John and Steve coming up the trail looking sullen.

"I guess I'll have to buy a new one," Steve said, turning back to look once again at the thicket.

As he turned, I glimpsed orange up under the folded-down hood of his sweatshirt. His license hadn't fallen off, but just flipped up under the hood. We teased him mercilessly but only for a second since his son was there.

Across the road, we didn't find any birds, but something high up in a maple sapling caught my eye. "It's just a nest or something," John said as we walked up the trail. Even Maggie was dragging now since the crisp blue day had turned a little humid and warm, even with the comparatively cool air coming off the lake. But it wasn't a nest. I had been up and down this trail several times over the past couple of weeks, and this was something new and out of place. Once I was beneath it, the fur became clearly visible.

"What is it, Uncle Joey?" Eric called from the trail through the wall of brush.

"It's a raccoon."

"Somebody must have shot it," John offered. "It looks bloated."

Just then the monstrous coon turned his head and looked down at me, his eyes bright with mischief. His coat was thick and in prime condition, and he was easily five pounds heavier than any raccoon I'd ever seen in my life. The girls and I had been out coon hunting several times with no success, and I got excited, rattling on about

Maggie in hot pursuit.

how I had been "looking for one of these things," much to the snickering delight of my hunting companions. After snapping the leash on Maggie, I dropped the raccoon with a single blast from my shotgun. Following the progress of the critter from sky to ground with the barrel of my gun, I was ready for anything. Maggie began barking. Raccoon rain was not something she was used to seeing. Thankfully, it was dead when it hit the ground.

I was thrilled with the raccoon. Why? I don't know. I just was. I guess I am as much a big-game hunter as I am a bird hunter, and this was one *big* game animal. After carrying the coon proudly back to my truck, and straining under the weight, I was picked on for the remainder of the afternoon by Steve and John.

"That was really cool, Uncle Joey! Is that the biggest one you've ever seen?"

I love my nephew.

With Maggie picking up no bird sign (several theories were advanced about the size of the raccoon being related to the relative absence of the pheasants), we ventured off the trail. Steve reminded me that he and I had been in that general vicinity a few years ago, been turned around in the high thorns, and eventually had to climb several trees before finding our way out.

We laughed at the memory.

I would tell you about the rest of that day, but it mostly revolves around getting lost in the brush and having trouble finding our way out, and it's just not that interesting.

The Snipe Hunt

"Yeah, we had a good time," Greta said. "I got a rabbit and Joel got a snipe."

"Whoa," said Jobe, my future brother-in-law, holding up his hands and suddenly standing.

"No, really . . ." I began, defending Greta.

Jobe, shaking his head and still holding his hands up, left the room before I could utter another word. I could hear him back in the kitchen wondering in a mutter how stupid we really thought he was.

Well, I really *did* shoot a snipe, and that was only *part* of our day.

Greta and I had teamed up with Maggie and Ted for an early morning hunt in my hometown. It was nice to see both dogs back in top form and working as a true team instead of a tag team. Not far into the field, the dogs began bouncing around crazily in some ankle-deep water. Maggie moved out to the right and Ted to the left. A light fluttering of wings caused me to spin around. Caught off-balance, I watched the snipe rocket skyward as I fumbled with the safety. My second shot seemed to knock off some feathers and the bird slanted downward, still under power, into a far hedgerow.

"Woodcock?" Greta asked.

"Snipe."

Greta nodded. She'd seen me bring them home once or twice before. Unlike my soon-to-be brother-in-law later in the day, my wife at least believed me.

"Fetch it up," I said, motioning Ted to the hedgerow.

"You didn't hit it," Greta said, very matter-of-factly.

"Oh, yes I did. Fetch it up," I said, *more* matter-of-factly.

As Ted probed a tiny ditch that bisected the hedgerow, I prayed—*Please let me have hit it.* A moment later the big dog emerged with the tiny bird clenched in his jaws. I tried to be nonchalant about the whole thing.

"*Hmm*," Greta said as if she wasn't at all sure that the small bird was indeed the same one I'd shot at. Well, maybe Ted just happened to find a snipe that had died of old age that morning in that very patch of cover. I turned the little bird over in my hands, admiring the plumage. Smaller than a woodcock, the snipe has more striking, deeply striped markings. Everyone who has ever seen one while hunting with me has called it a woodcock. While woodcock are more likely to hang out in the woods, snipe are usually found in places exactly like the one from which this one had flushed. I'm not sure how abundant they are, but they must be fairly numerous because there is a hunting

Just one last sniff.

season for them. I've often seen them walking around the edges of mud puddles in late summer and early fall, like shorebirds that have lost their shore. If you can find three or four inches of water in a grassy field in October, you have a good chance of seeing some snipe. I think, too, that they are a little more odorous than woodcock since the dogs seem to have no difficulty in pinpointing them for a flush. Of course, this could have something to do with the relatively open areas in which they are found. I love the way they flush— straight up and then beelining for the next state, and occasionally coming back around for a peek at you. None of that "put every tree between me and you" business at which woodcock are so good. Snipe at least give you a chance.

Cutting across an adjoining field, we let the dogs drink for a moment or two at another ditch. I sat on a freshly cut stump while the dogs lounged. When Ted began showing some interest in a brushpile, I told Greta, "There's probably a rabbit in there."

As Ted bulldozed into one side of the pile, the rabbit zipped out the other, right in front of Greta. I watched two clumps of dirt kick up just shy of the rabbit as she fired her autoloader. The third shot may have hit the rabbit, but not hard enough to slow it down.

"I think I hit it," Greta said.

"You might have."

Far out of range, the rabbit made a hard right turn out of the hedgerow and, much to my surprise, headed for the dreadful ankle-twisting ruts in the next field— the same ones we had fruitlessly worked for pheasants on opening day. I had no yearning to go across that mess for a rabbit. Of course, Maggie had other thoughts.

When she crossed the scent trail where the rabbit had turned, it was as if someone lit her afterburners. Over the ruts she went, in a beeline for the far cornfield.

"Oh, no," I groaned. I would not have minded chasing a big ringneck across there, but the prospect of real physical harm just didn't seem worth it for a rabbit. Greta and I moved quickly up and down, through and over the horrible ruts, but Maggie easily outdistanced us. Halfway across, I held up my hand and said, "If that rabbit gets to the cornfield, we're never going to have a shot. Let's whistle Maggie in if we can and go back to the field for birds."

"I think I hit it. I had to have hit it."

Like Maggie, Greta was determined.

"If you hit it and it went this far, it has to be the toughest rabbit I ever saw."

Just at that moment, the unmistakable squall of a dying cottontail carried over the field from somewhere eighty or ninety yards to our north. And here came Maggie, carefully cradling the rabbit.

"Jeez," Greta said. "Do you think I shot it? I mean, she couldn't just catch it—not on dry ground. She caught that one in the snow last year, I know, but. . . ."

"You never know with her," I said, smiling, as Maggie came slowly up the field with the big gray cottontail drooping across her jaws.

Once Maggie was back, completely spent and out of breath, she handed Greta the rabbit. My quick postmortem revealed that Greta had hit it with a few pellets. But still, you gotta love that Maggie. Two hundred yards she had gone, hot on that rabbit's trail— *two hundred!*

Since we were halfway there, we worked in and around the corn for an hour or more looking for our original quarry, a rooster pheasant, but didn't put up a bird.

Unless you count that make-believe snipe, of course.

I Told You I'd Be Back, Mr. Pheasant

Bleary-eyed from working late the night before, I went through the mechanical preparations of getting ready to hunt: I filled the dog's water jug and my water bottle; I loaded my vest with the few Number 6 shotshells I had left; I found the hat and whistle and pulled on my brush pants—if not enthusiastically, then at least hopefully.

I was ready to go get some pheasants, and I knew just the spot—the same place I had gone with Joe the other day. A big, wily, taunting rooster with my name on him lived there, and I intended to get him this time.

Half-awake now, thanks to the three cups of coffee I'd chugged while stumbling around the house looking for my gear, I checked the hunting regulations and verified that woodcock season ended today. I would make a special point of going through the dogwood thicket Joe and I had worked. (My ears still seemed to ring occasionally from the missed shots, but I am not easily deterred when it comes to birds.) Yes, we'd left plenty of birds for next time— and now it *was* next time. I was hustling to finish the preparations when Greta said, "Honey, have you looked outside?"

I hadn't. Then it dawned on me that the kids and Greta had been sitting by the radio listening to school closings and delays for the past few minutes. *School closings?* Was it an early November snowstorm? Was my truck buried up to its axles? Would I have to dig out the plow for the ATV before I could get out to hunt? So I looked outside.

Fog, and lots of it.

Thinking back to the previous evening, I vaguely remembered the shimmering white waves coming off the fields as I drove home from work. It had been rolling in then, but I hadn't made much of it. Now it had made quite a bit of itself. From my front window I could not see the road thirty yards distant. In fact, though I could see the front license plate of my truck, I couldn't make out the rear end of the vehicle at all.

"School's delayed two hours," Greta announced.

"Wow."

We live in western New York, where school isn't usually closed or delayed until it gets so bad that the snowplows need to be plowed out. And they were delaying for *fog*? It must be bad out there.

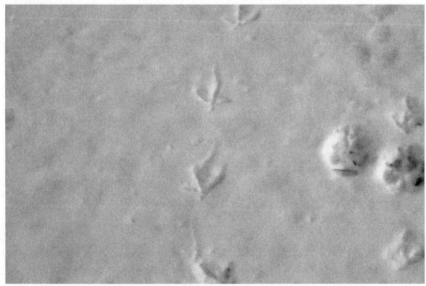

Pheasant tracks, followed by bird-dog tracks.

"OK, I better leave now then."

"Are you sure you don't want to wait till it clears out a little?" Greta asked.

I kissed her and the girls and left before my sanity could come into question. On the road, with Maggie pacing back and forth in the bed, I began questioning it myself. Creeping along at ten miles an hour as I climbed up the ridge toward Pendleton, I'd see oncoming cars appear as if out of nowhere. One second there was thick fog, and the next, two dim headlights would rush past my truck at the probably unhealthy speed of twenty or even twenty-five miles an hour.

People are awfully reckless sometimes.

By the time I reached the fields, none of the fog had lifted. I felt as if I was floating in another dimension as cars went by out on the road, heard but unseen. I sat on the tailgate with Maggie as the sun came up (well, I assumed it was coming up—the day was getting brighter) and waited for the fog to lift. There was no sense in going out yet since the sound of a flushing rooster would be nothing more than an invisible frustration—not to mention the potential of having some other hunter unload on a bird from the other side of a field and pepper me with Number 6s.

No, thanks.

Within a half-hour I could make out saplings at the field's edges and see the ground nearby. The fog had lifted twenty or thirty feet in the air, giving the impression of a large, fluffy blanket that someone had used to tuck in the countryside.

"Let's go, Mag."

She had been whining quietly the whole time, anxious to be out of the truck, and when I finally unsnapped her leash, she was on fire. I thought she'd gotten on scent even before I had my gun loaded, but it was just one of those bursts of doggy energy she occasionally needs to blow out of her system. Finally she fell into a nice quartering pattern ahead of me, working even closer than usual, perhaps due to the fog. I didn't waste any time heading directly for the place Joe and I had seen that rooster. I realized that it had been a few days and that bird could have moved hundreds of yards or even miles by now. But all last night and this morning my dreams had focused on the small depression in the center of the field. If nothing else, it gave me a frame of reference and a little hope. At least I had seen a bird there once, and such things are most important in this kind of hunting. The more hope, the harder you are likely to hunt. A mind game? Maybe, but as any good deer hunter will tell you, it's a tactic that works.

I don't know what made me carry the side-by-side again. I couldn't hit anything with it this year—that much I had proven—but I still seemed drawn to my old gun instead of the new autoloader, with which I actually seemed able to hit things. So when the first critter, a rabbit, darted out of a brushpile that Maggie had begun molesting, I swung with the fleeing bunny and pulled the trigger, but missed. I quickly found the back trigger and the second barrel roared . . . missed again! At the sound, the rabbit stopped dead in its tracks, giving me ample time for a third shot, which, of course, I did not have.

The rabbit did not wait for me to reload.

Dejectedly breaking open the scratched old gun, I slid in two more shells with that satisfying *thonk-thonk* that all double shotgunners know so well. The sound seemed strange and muted in the shroud of mist and fog. I was either lost in thought or still not fully awake

Rooster pheasant in a nasty thicket.

(a much better excuse for my shooting) when something caused me to snap out of it and realize that Maggie was no longer with me. She hadn't come back at the sound of my shot at the rabbit, come to think of it, and that was not like her.

Uh-oh.

I listened intently through the swirling mist and heard the tinkling of collar tags off to my left. Along with that came the distinct sounds of sniffing and snorting, starting and stopping in the long grass. *She's birdy,* I thought to myself as I began trotting in her direction.

Before I had gone ten steps, the fluttering of wings made me stop and instinctively raise my gun. The rooster didn't begin cackling until it was fifteen feet in the air and climbing quickly away from me. It was perhaps a bit too far out (darn me for not paying attention to Maggie), but I touched off both the front and the back triggers as fast as I could find them. The bird didn't even hesitate, flying for all it was worth toward the next hedgerow, straight out ahead of us about a hundred yards.

Maggie started after it at a full run, and I was surprised when I was able to call her back. Rather than taking the direct approach, I snapped the leash on her, and we swung wide around the end of the hedgerow about fifty yards from where I thought the bird had landed. I knew it would hit the ground and turn right or left and run like hell, so why should we bother doing what it *expected* us to do? I started at the far side and far end of the row. The tactic worked, but I had miscalculated. In my experience, wild birds rarely fly back to where you flushed them the first time. Normally they keep putting more and more real estate between you and them until they eventually wear you out. From a pheasant's point of view, it's a sound plan when it comes to evading foxes and coyotes. So, trying to be smarter than the average coyote, I went around the back. Maggie got on the scent right away. The bird *had* run all this way already.

We had him—only he didn't know that.

This time, the rooster flushed in the supposedly taboo direction—back the way it had come. Keeping the thick hedgerow as a protective screen between my gun and its tail feathers, it flew a good two hundred yards this time— thank God the fog was beginning to lift so I could see where it went. It flared its wings near a large, lone willow bush in the center of the field, an excellent landmark and one we jogged directly toward—no pussyfooting around.

No more *plans*.

The grass around the willow was stifling and long, and the bird would have a hard time trying to run out ot there. We went right in for the kill. Maggie, thirty yards ahead of me, sprang through the grass like she was walking on the Sea of Tranquillity (a spot on the moon—low gravity and all that). I, too, was ready, although I did pop my gun open once just to make sure I had put a couple of fresh shells in there. (I *still* wasn't quite awake.)

When Maggie closed the last yards to the base of the tree, I knew the end game was here. She became certifiably insane on the scent of the big bird. I half lifted my gun as she closed the last few feet. When the bird went up on the far side of the bush, it flew another hundred yards, always keeping the bush between us. This bird was a survivor. Locking its wings, it flared and landed inside the woodcock thicket I had hoped to hit later on. The bird had definitely earned the right to live another day.

Naturally, we went right after him.

I wish I could say we found that rooster again, but we didn't. He pulled a vanishing act that would do credit to other big, wild birds I'd chased over the years. I don't know how they do it—how they elude a nose as keen as Maggie's or Ted's—but they do. Once inside that thicket, the rooster had somehow managed to vanish. Thankfully, we did flush seven woodcock while trying to find him. It seemed fitting, this being the last day of woodcock season.

Of course, it would have seemed more fitting if I had managed to hit even *one* of them.

All Right, Let's Just Give It a Try

Even though much of the place had been hayed during opening week, I still wanted to try JK's place just once. He'd had the decency to leave a patch of scraggly corn up, even if he had laid the surrounding fields down to only knee-high cover with a few passes of the combine. I can't imagine that any of the stuff he cut was worth anything as livestock feed, but it could have been, since I know absolutely nothing about livestock other than how to outrun the bull steer that guards one of my favorite flyfishing holes in the Catskills. I'd been wanting to get back to JK's since the first week, figuring that any birds still on the property had probably taken up residence either in the hedgerows or in that little island oasis of corn.

Besides, with Greta and my two girls with me, the company was excellent. Jessica and Jennifer stayed dutifully back from Greta and me and talked the afternoon away. What a seven- and a ten-year-old can possibly find to talk about for hours on end is beyond me, but then again, I have never tried hard to delve into the workings of any female mind, no matter its age. I kept these thoughts to myself since Greta was armed. Ted trotted along, a rather serious look on his big, blocky face as he inspected the dismal cover of the cut fields. I didn't bother encouraging him to hunt very hard, hoping he would save his energy for the corn and the hedgerows.

I'd started the day hunting alone with Maggie, and it shames me to tell you that I shot my gun twelve times—no misprint there—at what I believe to be the same rooster that had humiliated me on two previous occasions. If I'd bothered to sit down to count, I believe I would have discovered that this bird had easily cost me a box of shells already. Fortunately, I'm relatively adept at creating mental blocks about such things, although my pounded shoulder and ringing ears were incontrovertible proof of my disastrous association with that bird. Once again today, we had flushed the rooster multiple times and always just at the far edge of my shotgun's reach. Maggie had come home exhausted, as had her master.

With Maggie and Ted once again playing tag team, I realized just how lucky I was to have two dogs this year. As we approached the first hedgerow, Ted burst into a trot, and I let him go. Greta followed closely behind him. Walking the row from east to west, we covered the whole thing without Ted kicking out even a rabbit.

We cut into the stunted, chest-high corn, and I hung back so Greta could get the first shot. I snickered as she repeatedly raised her shotgun when mourning doves flushed wildly from the cover, at least three dozen of them in explosive little groups of four or five. I remembered seeing them in here early in the season, the day we'd neglected to bring along the guns. It was easy to snicker even with the knowledge that if it had been me out in front, I'd have been twice as twitchy as she was. The flapping of a mourning dove lifting from the ground is surprisingly loud, a sound not unlike that of a flushing pheasant. Unfortunately, not even the corn, my ace-in-the-hole, produced a pheasant. We turned right out of the corn and into the next hedgerow, which was punctuated by several large piles of trees that had been removed from the fields and stacked haphazardly. It looked like rabbit heaven.

"Stay back, girls—way back," I said as Ted barreled into the brushpiles. I'd no sooner said it than a rabbit raced right between the girls and me. Once it was safely beyond them and racing up my side of the row, I shot three times in rapid succession (and vaguely heard the "Wow!" and "Cool!" from Jessica and Jennifer). The rabbit tripped at the third shot—from the sound of the concussions alone, I am sure—but picked itself back up and hustled for the promised land. Ducking back into the hedgerow, he was gone.

"Ted!" I yelled.

The Lab, panting with excitement, blasted out of the thick brush and ran along next to me until I reached the spot where the cottontail had ducked back in. He picked up the scent immediately. I could see Greta coming up the hedgerow on the other side.

"Get ready!" I told her.

Once again the rabbit came out on my side, four feet in the air if it was an inch. I let it get out a bit to avoid pulverizing it and shot, tumbling it for good. Looking down, I realized it was a good thing I'd hit it because I had just exhausted the last shell in my gun. Quickly stuffing three more in, I called for Ted to fetch the rabbit, but he refused to come out. Still intently sniffing the spot from which he had successfully flushed the critter, he just wanted to revel in the smell for a while, I guessed.

Wrong. (As a side note here, I fervently hope you have not been counting the number of times I have been wrong in this book. If you *have* been, stand by for more.)

The second rabbit came out with an acrobatic hop that put the first rabbit's to shame. Ted was in the air right behind it, so I didn't shoot. Cutting the corner into a perpendicular hedgerow with astonishing speed, dog and cottontail crashed into the cover. Ted sounded like a derailed locomotive with all the snapping and cracking he was making. I could see the saplings in the hedgerow parting with his progress. Greta and I trotted along on opposite sides of the hedgerow.

The hedge terminated in another massive pile of trees that had grown up with berry bushes and other assorted nasties. I remembered seeing the pile last winter when Dad and I had hunted out here—it had been littered with bunny tracks. There were countless holes up under the branches, and I knew that once the rabbit got in there, it would take some major excavation to get him out. Even Blockhead Ted probably wouldn't be up to the task.

"I see him," Greta said.

"Ted?" I asked.

"Where's Ted?" she asked.

"He's back here by me."

I was confused. The girls and I jumped at the unexpectedness of her shot, and Ted leaped into the thorns and briars as if he were swan-diving into a cool swimming pool.

"Fetch it, Teddy, come on," Greta said. "No! Right there! Ted!"

Uncharacteristically, he couldn't find it. Greta finally picked the rabbit up herself, shaking her finger at Ted.

Back at the truck, I asked the girls if they'd had fun. According to them, it was *really cool* that Mommy and Daddy each got a rabbit. But it would have been *awesome* if we each had shot a pheasant.

Amen.

Timing Is Everything

The field looked much like it had the first time I was here with my father, when we finally killed the first wild bird on that Thursday of opening week. This time, though, the sun, instead of peeking in from below a ribbon of black clouds in the east, battled the gray skies of the west. Orange and pink streamers streaked the underside of the heavy clouds, possibly laden with the first flurries of the year if the forecaster was right. This day was similar to that Thursday in one other way: I didn't have my camera.

I just never learn.

Glad to be out of work for the day, Brian pushed slightly ahead of me as we followed behind the slow-working Ted. I'm sure Brian would have much preferred the faster pace set by his beloved Maggie, but she needed a rest. I wasn't even sure she could have gotten into the truck this afternoon. I, too, was lame. Rather than hunt birds early that day, I'd ridden my ATV out to a far tree stand and bowhunted the morning away, enjoying the sight of a doe and two fawns feeding around below me for the better part of two hours. I decided then, as I rested my burning legs and arthritic toe, that there are definite advantages to hunting both birds and deer in their concurrent seasons. By late afternoon, when Brian finally managed to get out of work, I was fairly well rested.

The cool air came directly from the north, and as we headed that way, Ted quartered in a tight, choppy cadence, never venturing more than fifteen or twenty yards to the left or right before slicing back the other way. Accustomed to his more laid-back style, I began wondering if he was on scent. In the ankle-deep water where we'd flushed and killed the snipe, almost predictably a snipe went up. Brian followed it up with his gun, asking, "What is it? Woodcock?"

"Snipe. Honest."

With the close of woodcock season yesterday, snipe and rail had also closed, so I was thankful he hadn't shot first and asked questions later. Conservation officers tend to frown upon the poaching of federally regulated migratory birds, a category covering both snipe and woodcock.

"What's the season on them?" Brian asked.

"Ended yesterday."

A moment later, with Ted still hustling around and kicking up a spray of cold water ahead of him, another snipe went up.

We worked the entire field, not bothering to venture into the woodcock cover where we had enjoyed so much action this year. There was no frost yet, and I had no doubt that the saplings were chock-full of timberdoodles, but why waste the time and suffer the frustration? Undoubtedly we would see more birds than we had ever before laid eyes on. It *always* works that way. At the end of the field, we cut across it diagonally, kicking up yet another common snipe, which circled us three times, peeping in defiance with each orbit. No pheasants, though— a condition on which Brian remarked not for the first time that afternoon.

Pheasant sneaking away through the grass.

"My dad and I shot the first one of the year over in that gray stuff," I said, motioning to the adjoining field.

"Let's go," Brian said, already turning in that direction. He did not want to waste a second, lacking the luxury of taking most of bird season as vacation time, as I had. Crossing through the dogwood hedgerow, we waded into the odd, chest-deep stuff. Last time we'd been through here, the mud had sucked at our feet, but now the ground was ice-firm as the thermometer had spent much of the past forty-eight hours considerably lower than 32 degrees. Ted was back to his usual slow-working pace and was difficult to see below the dense canopy of the odd, dried vegetation.

Looking back toward the low sun, I realized I had a picture similar to this scene. On my first recon trip out here earlier in the year to snoop on the whereabouts of the wild ringnecks, Maggie and Ted had flushed some roosters. The blurry photo of one of them sailing over that hedgerow hung on the bulletin board over my desk. I mentioned it to Brian as incentive.

"It's probably the one you and your dad shot," he said pessimistically.

"There's more than one. Trust me."

"Never."

We crisscrossed the field east to west and north to south, and finally south to north again, letting the wind do the work for Ted, who, surprisingly enough, wasn't favoring his eye in the slightest and still seemed to have ample energy. Good Old Ted was back.

Just as the bottom edge of the sun burned into the treetops, Good Old Ted kicked it into high gear. Snorting and sniffing around in circles for a frantic moment, he finally took off north, running straight into the wind with his nose down. Brian and I trotted after him. Where the field gave way to a small mowed patch, Ted broke into a hard run across the open ground. Just when it appeared that he was going to dive into the next patch of the weird gray stuff, he turned and ran east along the mowed patch. I could easily picture a big old rooster pheasant doing just that—the unpredictable. Suddenly, though, where the gray field butted against the big rutted field where Maggie had caught Greta's rabbit, Ted stopped, appearing to lose interest.

It was as if the scent had just faded away. Could the bird have flushed wild and we just hadn't seen it? No. This section of the county is as flat as an oak plank. We would have seen a rising bird. Could it have been a rabbit? I don't think so—not with the way Ted was acting.

Where arrrre you, Mr. Pheasant?

"What now?" Brian asked, well aware of the fading daylight.

"Watch Ted for a minute."

Unfortunately, all Ted did was watch *us* for direction.

OK, let's think about this, I thought (even though I really knew better than to try to outthink a wild pheasant). He probably hadn't cut back on us, with all the noise we were making. So there was no sense in our wasting time where we had already been. He may have gone straight into the next field, and Ted was catching old scent from a rabbit or a different bird. Not likely, since I had long ago learned not to doubt the dogs' noses. That left one alternative— that the pheasant had merely hopped (perhaps literally) from the open mowed patch into the next field of thick, nasty stuff. *If I were a bird*, I dared to think, *that's where I'd go to hide from a big dog and two armed men.* With little fanfare or explanation to Brian, I steered Ted into the thick gray stuff in the next field, and we began zigzagging back and forth, finally cutting far to the north and walking out the field to its termination at a piece of private property.

Nothing.

With the sun nearly gone now, we started back through the field. We'd already covered it once, and it would have been nice to walk up one of the better footpaths along its edge instead of fighting the grabby foliage, but if we had learned one thing over the years, it was that persistence pays. And Brian and I were persistent, if nothing else, when it came to wild birds.

We didn't say much. Both of us were disappointed, Brian more so than I; we had fervently hoped that Ted's burst of birdiness would end in a shot at a pheasant. Watching the Lab work slowly along to my right, barely quartering at all and showing signs of tiring, I knew that wasn't going to happen tonight.

"Joel!" Brian whispered as he came to an abrupt stop to my right.

"What's wrong?"

"He's right here."

"Who."

"The *bird.*"

"Rooster?"

"Big."

"Walk him up."

"Want to send Ted after him?"

"No, just flush him before he runs."

Brian took another step, and the bird went up. I hesitated for a moment, then shot. Pheasant feathers rained over Ted and me, the finer ones blowing south on the increasing breeze.

"Why didn't you shoot?" Brian asked.

"What?"

"The bird! He was right in front of you."

"Why didn't *you* shoot?"

"I did."

We *both* did, again.

We let Ted retrieve the rooster, to the accompaniment of considerable bad-mouthing from Brian about the dog's scenting abilities. I defended Ted, though, explaining that it had been his intention all along to corral the bird into that one small corner of the field and. . . .

Well, you get the picture.

Diagnosis: Neurosis

I would like to say that I awoke with grand thoughts of golden fields and azure skies, but it was nothing like that. My sole thought was, *Today, you are going to get yours.* I was going back after that rooster once more. I knew he would probably flush wild again, driving Ted and Joe and me crazy. But short of buying an 8-gauge shotgun and loading it with buckshot the size of cannonballs, I knew there was only one way I was going to get that bird.

Persistence.

With Maggie still not quite herself from the *last* time we'd gone after that critter and Ted healthier than he'd been all season, Ted got the call. Though a bit stiff at first from his rabbit-chasing endeavors a day earlier, he had enthusiasm enough for all three of us. Also, I thought his longer legs might be an advantage against this bird that seemed to use every trick in the book. If nothing else, maybe Ted could *outrun* it. Now, you may well be saying, *How do you know it was the same bird? Isn't it possible there were two or even three birds in that general area that caused you those three individual cases of indigestion?* Sure, there was a good population of birds around there, and sure, it was possible. But I doubt it. I think it was the same bird—a pheasant with *smarts.*

In short, a *trophy* bird.

Joe and I made several different approaches to the area. Joe, along as a guest, probably didn't have any clue to what I was doing, but each time we circled a field or sneaked up on a hedgerow, we did it in a way I had meticulously formulated in my head since my last visit here. I had put on my deer-hunting thinking cap and was strategizing like someone trying to outwit a sneaky old white-tailed buck. The goal was to give the bird a good mix of my own unpredictability and a lethal dose of careful planning. I did not want *him* outguessing *us* this time.

We started by approaching the roosting cover where Joe had originally shot at the bird, hunting *with* the wind and then turning abruptly *into* the wind, then with the wind again, then letting Ted get his nose back into the wind. When that failed, we gave one edge of the woods a thorough blanketing, working the dog back and forth across it five times.

OK, so you're roosting in the hedgerows.

We sneaked up on the hedgerows. We worked them upwind, and then we worked them downwind. We cut into them and back out of them. I even walked up the center of them, hoping to shag the bird free with all my crashing and breaking. Nothing happened.

Finally, to the fields.

Back and forth and back again, with the wind and into the wind and across the wind, quartering with the wind from every possible angle. Apparently Joe didn't mind what was starting to look like the hunting equivalent of beating a dead horse. If he did mind, he was polite enough not to say so. When I looked at my watch, four hours had passed and we had hunted essentially the same sixty or seventy acres for that entire time.

"What do you think?" I asked.

"I'm ready for lunch."

"Me too."

I didn't quite want to quit yet but realized how neurotic I must have appeared and thought I could cover myself by being willing to stop to *eat.* If I had been by myself, I'd probably still have been out there at dinnertime—a fact that perhaps proves the neurosis diagnosis.

Walking back up the same mowed tractor path we'd come in on, we detoured off it to take a more direct route back to my truck. Ted, his tongue dragging even on this cool morning, was lagging behind.

"Come on, Ted."

"Maybe he's on something, Joel."

"I think he's just worn out."

Ted had his nose buried in a big clump of switchgrass but wasn't acting very interested. It was just his nature to sniff things. I refrained from calling him again when Joe, walking back toward him, began poking at the long bunches of grass with the toe of his boot.

A rooster erupted from that tiny wedge of space between Joe and Ted. *Got you now,* I thought, smiling and knowing Joe's proclivity to hit what he aims at. I didn't even raise my gun. It all seemed to happen in slow motion: the rooster breaking from a crouch and springing into the flush, Ted jumping into the air behind it, Joe's gun coming up, the tiny *tink* of the safety catch on Joe's gun coming off, then . . . then . . . *silence.* The flapping of wings; no shooting.

In a spasm, I lifted my own shotgun and began blazing away at the retreating bird with real passion, thinking, *No, not again!* On the third shot, the bird came down and Ted pounced on it at once. I turned to look at Joe, and judging by his reaction, my gaze was probably something less than ordinary.

"Jeez, Joel. Sorry . . . I . . ."

"What happened?"

"Ted was there. I didn't want to shoot him."

"Oh, that's fine."

Though Ted had been on the ground and the bird twenty feet in the air, I respected Joe's efforts to protect my dog from harm. So, was it the same bird we had chased around there before? No. Sorry. It would make a nice ending to the story, but it couldn't have been. Granted, that pheasant's willingness to sit there in the grass and let two men and a dog walk within spitting distance of it—not once but *twice*—was cagey and unquestionably worthy of respect. But that other bird? No, I am certain the bird that made the long walk back to the truck in the back of my game vest was not the cagey rooster that had cost me so much in shotshell reloading supplies this year.

He's still out there.

A Great Day, A Good Year

I had one day of vacation left before late November, when I would happily depart for opening week of deer season in the Catskills. The reports were rolling in about the bucks going into rut, and I was more than a little tempted to spend my last day of vacation relaxing in one of my tree stands high above the forest floor.

But that would be too easy.

Knowing my bird hunting would now be relegated to weekends and a few stolen hours after work, I felt like I had better get Maggie out one more time. She'd fully recovered from her encounters with the evil rooster, and so had I—other than a hard feeling or two. Heading once again for the ridge, I watched in the rearview as Maggie paced excitedly back and forth under the cap. Her smile was unmistakable, as was mine. With low clouds crowding in overhead, the day was not deep or blue and the fields weren't bright gold. It wasn't a picture-perfect day by any means. It was just a plain old day, like most hunting days. But Maggie and I were excited enough to ignore the impending rain. I could tell from the parked cars that

Maggie and late season pheasant.

Jim and Bill, a couple of guys I knew from the club, were out on the property, and I parked well away from them and headed out to the far fields. Maggie bounced like a gazelle through the long grass, with no apparent traces of stiffness.

Being a sentimental type of guy (no, really—*work* with me here) I made it a point as we walked out the tractor path to mentally recount the events of the past weeks. Despite the growing scarcity of places to hunt and the steady march of development across the county, it had been a good year. There were many things I had to be thankful for. Interrupting my thoughts, Maggie woofed—more of a terse growl, really—and a rooster was in the air in front of me. Miraculously, it dropped at my first shot.

"Good girl!" I said as she carried the bird to me. It was a beautiful specimen, all bright colors and long, trailing tail feathers. What a way to end the season! Maybe we would even get another bird. Wouldn't that just be the capper? Maggie, still with fine ringneck back-feathers poking out from one corner of her mouth, began working even harder, hopping and pouncing and jumping, smiling and nub-wagging the whole time. She was even happier to be out than I was. It was as if she, too, realized that this was the last big hunt. When she started getting birdy again, I began having delusions of grandeur. If I managed to kill two birds, I would have to hunt down Bill and Jim just to show them—out of courtesy, of course.

But it wasn't another bird. Maggie began a hard dash down-field, stopping suddenly and making several small circles. I half-raised the shotgun and tried to douse the smug smile that leaked out all over my face. A bird was about to go up.

"Come on, Maggie, make it a rooster—not a hen, a *rooster*," I chanted.

Maggie froze in the grass, her nose down and her paws held tightly together in front of her. Suddenly, her head jabbed forward like a mongoose taking a poke at a cobra. The resulting wail from the grass below her was a familiar and not at all surprising sound. With a relatively gentle grip, she held the rabbit. By the time she carefully dropped it at my feet, it had stopped kicking. Maggie's mouth was a mess of feathers and rabbit fur. This time I remembered the camera and snapped a picture of my goofy little dog after praising her unique skills once again.

"Good girl!"

She knew it.

Before we had covered another hundred yards—my heart still hadn't slowed much since the first flush—I heard a rooster cackling back in the square patch of dogwoods where I'd missed so many woodcock last week. Maggie heard it, too, and began running in that direction. Before I could blow the whistle in an admittedly pointless attempt to slow her down, a shotgun blast boomed from the thicket, followed quickly by another. The rooster came out of the dogwoods flying in my direction. It spotted me at the last moment and veered wide, swinging around us a hundred yards off and locking its wings before sailing back into the hedgerow. I would like to say I wasn't tempted to go after it, but I was. I recognized Jim's voice yelling something I couldn't make out. A moment later, his springer appeared near the edge of the thicket, scanning the skies for the wayward bird. Jim was right behind him.

"Hey, Joel! Did it go down out here?"

I pointed.

"It went *that far?* I blew the feathers off it. It has to be dead."

"I don't know, Jim . . . the way it was flying."

"Really. I hit him pretty good."

I gave him specific directions and landmarks to where it had landed, and he and his dog rapidly beelined up the field, disappearing at nearly the right point in the hedge. His dog was good. If the bird was there, the springer would find it. I had to restrain Maggie for the next few moments, explaining why we could not go after the rooster. She had trouble understanding. I had to physically pick her up and point her in the opposite direction before she would begin hunting for me again without trying to sneak back toward where that bird had gone. Don't let anyone tell you that dogs don't remember things, especially *important* things like where birds land.

Two hours later, we were ready to call it a morning—and a season, for all practical purposes. I tried to block from my mind the thought of tomorrow's workday, but work thoughts are nearly as persistent as bird dogs. I also knew I should get home and do all of the things I'd neglected for the past month before normal day-to-day life consumed me once again. On the way out, Maggie insisted on making a right turn precisely where Jim's bird had locked wings. It had been hours ago and she had not forgotten. I let her go, stopping and letting the first few drops of rain cool my face as I listened to the familiar jingling of her tags down in the brush near the ditch. Finally tiring of her pigheaded persistence, I whistled softly.

She came back—carrying a dead rooster.

When she dropped it in my outstretched hand, the bird was still warm—Jim's bird, undoubtedly. Examining it closely, I saw it had indeed been hit. It was hard to believe it had gone that far.

"You are one good girl, Maggie."

She knew.

Bill and Jim were standing out on the main trail as if waiting for me.

Approaching them, I asked, "How did you two do?"

"Two," Bill said, patting his vest. "Hell of a good day."

"I just had those shots, when I saw you," Jim said.

Bill began teasing me. "Well, I heard Jimmy shoot twice. And I only heard one other shot, Joel. Slow day?"

Very slowly, I pulled off my vest and dumped the heavy contents—two huge roosters and the rabbit—at Bill's feet.

An old familiar bird hunting scene, with a new housing development.

Patting Maggie's head, I said, "This is one good dog."

Picking up one rooster, I handed it to Jim. "That's yours," I said.

He began laughing.

"This," I said, picking up the other cockbird, "is mine— the shot you heard."

Then I picked up the rabbit.

"Who got that one?" he asked.

I patted Maggie on the head again. "*This* is Maggie's."

"You took two birds and a rabbit and only used *one* shell?" Bill asked, laughing and smacking his knee. "Now *that* is one amazing day."

You can say that again.

TAILFEATHERS

Posted land, uncooperative landowners, ditch-to-ditch farming, uncontrolled predators. I'm afraid the problems I experience during my efforts to hunt wild birds in our vanishing countryside are not unique. In our nation, particularly in those increasingly scarce uplands east of the Mississippi River, the steady march of development is ringing in a new and uncharted era for birds and bird hunters. Problems with property owners, ecologically insensitive farming methods, and the profusion of foxes, coyotes, and raccoons (thank you, anti-fur people) are doing what two hundred years of hard hunting could not—steadily eradicating wild ringneck pheasant populations.

There is, however, hope.

What can we do? We can talk to farmers, explaining how intact hedgerows help prevent soil erosion and provide game habitat. We can plead our case to those people sitting on the fence in the uproar these days over hunting and trapping. And perhaps most important, we can join groups like Pheasants Forever, Ducks Unlimited, the Ruffed Grouse Society, and the like. Any group interested in preserving habitat for future generations of game and sportsmen will work for the benefit of those magnificent jungle-colored game birds we love. And as any tired, burr-covered bird dog will tell you, ringneck pheasants are certainly worthy of our protection and respect.

A long grass field without pheasants is an awfully empty place.